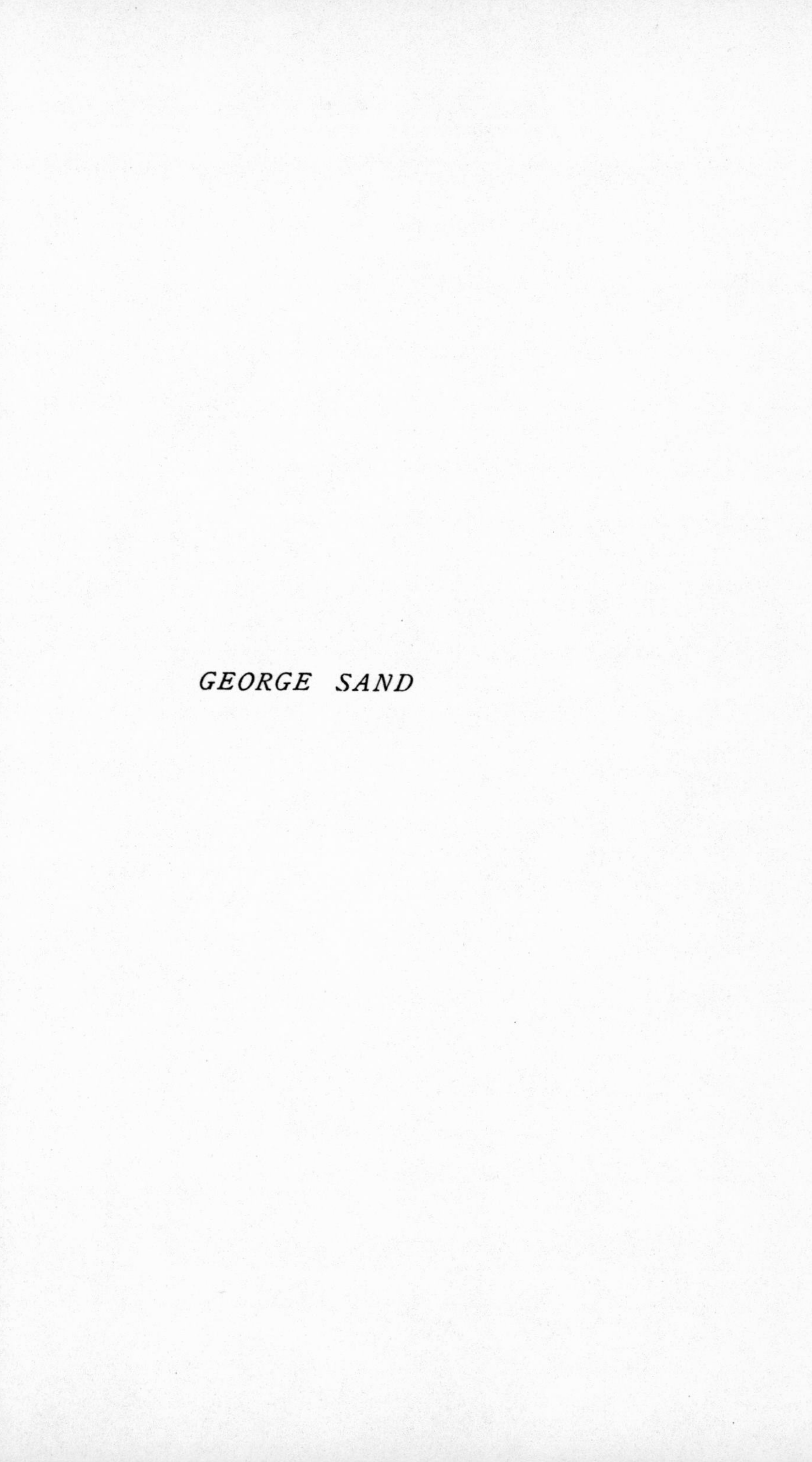

GEORGE SAND

GEORGE SAND

REPRODUCTION OF THE DRAWING BY COUTURE.

GEORGE SAND

BY THE LATE

ELME MARIE CARO

Member of the French Academy

Translated by

GUSTAVE MASSON, B.A. UNIV. GALLIC.,

KENNIKAT PRESS
Port Washington, N. Y./London

GEORGE SAND

First published in 1888
Reissued in 1970 by Kennikat Press
Library of Congress Catalog Card No: 76-103173
SBN 8046-0810-5

Manufactured by Taylor Publishing Company Dallas, Texas

TRANSLATOR'S PREFACE.

IT is easy now, in England at any rate, to form a true, a calm, and an impartial opinion of George Sand ; twenty-five years ago it would have been difficult ; half a century ago it would have been impossible. Time has the privilege of toning down all exaggerations, and of softening in a picture the colours which seemed to us, at first, false from their very brilliancy. We are astonished now at finding ourselves comparatively unmoved by the novels which, when they originally appeared, excited so powerfully our enthusiasm or our surprise ; and we have been led to judge from the purely literary point of view, books supposed to contain the programme of new and startling doctrines on philosophy, religion, and life in general.

M. Caro's biographical sketch of George Sand is, in every respect, the most satisfactory help to an appreciation of that wonderful character ; it is an important chapter in the literary history of an epoch which has witnessed the most complete transformation ever seen of French society in all its relations and aspects.

January, 1888.

GEORGE SAND.

CHAPTER I.

THE CHILDHOOD AND YOUTH OF GEORGE SAND.

IT is said that no one now reads George Sand. This may be so; but we believe that, if only in honour to the French language, there will be a reaction in favour of her works, or of those, at least, which time has purified and the consensus of taste distinctly set apart—those which are beyond the caprice and uncertainty of opinion. When we were asked to collect our reminiscences of this author, and revive them for these singularly indifferent and forgetful times, the request chimed in with a secret desire of our own to recall and give life to our impressions of days gone by, correcting and modifying them by comparison and acquired experience. Sand! this magic word brought back to me days of delicious dreaming and passionate discussion; it represented so many generous feelings, confused aspirations, and daring thoughts—such deep discouragements, such superhuman hopes mingled with the refined torture of doubt! This individual existence, this individual imagination was the type of a generation which vaguely tormented itself in the midst of the apparent quiet and prosperity that reigned as the year 1848 drew near; as if the rather monotonous course of events had produced a yearning for something else, an eager desire for emotion, an irresistible longing for the unknown both in facts and in ideas;—a generation, nevertheless, contented in the main, notwithstanding its undefined presentiments. Ardent though shadowy ideas of social reform or renovation lurked in many a mind thus unaccountably disquieted. There were times when a young man "suffering from the torment of the divine," as George Sand says, could in the same day hear one of Lacordaire's magnificent appeals at Notre-Dame, and Rachel's soul-stirring voice in some grand tragedy at the Théâtre-Français, or there also be enraptured with a perfect rendering of Alfred de Musset's exquisite and rhythmical prose—he might read some grand deep poem of Victor Hugo on the recent death of his daughter, discuss the merit of some sketch in Lamartine's *Girondins*, or lose himself in the wondrous charm of that gem in rustic poetry, *la Mare au Diable*, which by its loveliness has redeemed the prolix error of the *Meunier d'Angibault*.

These times, thus saturated with ideas and emotions, were strangely characterised by one of the great poets, who announced that "France was suffering from dulness," and who, even more strangely, persuaded her to believe it,—mistaking for dulness the prevailing fermentation and the discontent with the present, which did not satisfy the insatiable craving for excitement.

I speak especially of the already distant years 1846 and 1847, because in them George Sand's influence and glory culminated. What a stormy glory surrounds her name! The passionate controversies of which it was the occasion or the pretext are not yet forgotten; and indeed it is not wonderful that this brilliant and tempestuous fame should have called forth extravagant enthusiasm both in admiration and depreciation. On this subject few minds were capable of forming an impartial judgment. Here a species of judicial, if somewhat vindictive fury against the daring reformer would prevail; there a lyrical idolatry, such as characterised the works which were its object, and a vociferous chorus in honour of ideas and principles, confounded in an unreasoning apotheosis with the power of the inspiration and the beauty of the style. But these passions died long ago, and in presence of the real or affected indifference now professed about George Sand, not only a calmer judgment, but wider and perhaps more reasonable admiration are possible. And if it is true that this passionate partisanship has ceased because she is forgotten—nay, that the very works which were once the subject of such ardent discussion are no longer read, this study will still possess the merit that belongs to the discovery and exploration of unknown or unremembered regions.

From that date 1847 let us go back fifteen or sixteen years—towards the end of the winter of 1831—when George Sand, with some very light luggage, her little girl's cradle, and some manuscript written at Nohant amid the noise of children, arrived in Paris, where she found herself absolutely without friend or support in the world of letters. A vast desert of men of whom many were redoubtable competitors armed for the fray, and prepared to defend against the new-comer all means of access to editor, journal, and review. I have often tried to imagine the state of the Baronne Aurore Dudevant's mind when, at the age of twenty-seven, a voluntary fugitive from husband and home, and utterly unconscious of her powers, she resolved to bid defiance to the future, and to attempt in self-defence, and possibly also for the instruction of others, the solution of the great question of the absolute independence of women. How complex a nature was this, and how opposite the influences which had helped to form it! Who, seeing her at work in her garret on the Quai Saint-Michel, wrapped in a thick coat of coarse grey cloth, or following her as she accompanied her Berrichon friends to the restaurant Pinson, to the *estaminet*, to museums, concerts, and the pit of theatres on first-nights, would have recognised in the rather turbulent student—so eagerly curious about every literary and political occurrence of the clubs and the streets, about everything which occupied the attention of the intelligent youth of the day—the mystic pupil of the English convent, Sister Alicia's sweet and humble friend, or the shepherdess of Berry, adventurous and dreamy child of heath and wood? This knowing youth, who sets forth so gaily as evening draws on to perambulate the Quartier-Latin with his comrades, under the guidance of the very vain and very elderly young man, Henri Delatouche, the leader of the contemporary literary Bohemia,—this roving observer, this prentice-novelist, is a deeply earnest woman who has known unutterable sadness, who has lived by suffering, if indeed suffering can give life, and whose dearest affections and closest ties have become—by the fatality of circumstances, and that other fatality which each one bears within him, and of which he is the indefatigable and cruel artist—the cause of her acutest pain. She comes to Paris to begin life afresh, in defiance of opinion and the instincts of her sex, and as if with the object of persuading nature herself to co-operate in her design, *virilises* as far as possible her manner of life, dress, tastes, opinions, and talent. From among the numberless doctrines which circulate in the world she will adopt those which encourage hope in the future of humanity. She possesses and will bring into play an insatiable intellectual curiosity, and the generous and ungovernable impatience which is given by a sense of the absolute—admitting no possibility of evading a truth once accepted.

Even at the age of twenty-seven, how many regions of ideas has she not explored! yet she has found naught to satisfy or arrest her attention. Like Wilhelm Meister, she can count the years of her apprenticeship,—and what a hard one it has been! That exact itinerary, the *Hisoire de ma Vie*,* enables us to follow her through these

* Her grandmother was the daughter of Marshal Saxe and of a lady of the Verrière family, rather notorious in the

years—pointing out more than one rugged pathway, and discovering the hidden sources of her imagination.

For its principal source we must go back to her earliest infancy. George Sand's whole life was coloured by the influence which surrounded her cradle.

At once a child of the people through her mother, and a child of the aristocracy through her father, she ascribes her chief instincts to this peculiarity of her birth, athwart two classes, as she expresses it, to her love for her mother,—a love constantly hurt and wounded by prejudices felt long before they could have been understood; to her unreasoning affection for her father, an insurgent and romantic being, who in the heyday of youth and passion, and when in quest of the ideal, had abandoned himself, during a pause in his military life, to an exclusive and unequal love which involved him in a struggle with aristocratic principles and received ideas as em-

eighteenth century. Her grandfather was the celebrated M. Dupin de Francueil (called Francueil only by Jean-Jacques Rousseau and Madame d'Epinay), who at the age of sixty-two was still a charming if rather faded representative of the eighteenth century. Of their marriage was born a son, Maurice, who chose the career of a soldier, and was somewhat reckless. He was a brilliant talker with the pen. Very early in life he attached himself to a milliner in Paris, who was both amiable and intelligent. Madame Dupin was deeply incensed at this step, and though she relented at times, never quite forgave it. In 1804 a child was born to Maurice Dupin, a daughter—Aurore—who was subsequently known to the world as George Sand.

bodied in his family; lastly, to an alternately philosophical and religious education, and to the violent contrasts which life had presented to her from her infancy. Her character was moulded amid the conflicts which the blood of the people stirred up in her heart and life—"and if, later on, certain books affected her, it was because their tendencies merely confirmed and strengthened her own." If we add to the irresistible sense of solidarity and inheritance the painful heart-searchings which exposed her to such cruel misunderstanding,—if we add that she was perpetually the object of her mother's anger or her grandmother's ill-concealed contempt, we shall have shown something of the process which formed this ardent though often forcibly repressed nature, this true child of Paris, imbued with the prejudices of a race to which she only half belonged, and we shall also have explained the reason of her bitterness against the class-divisions which had made her childhood a time of such cruel suffering. Hence her instincts of equality and democracy, as she called them later—instincts which were but the outcome of an old and secret pain. From this point of view the earlier chapters of the *Histoire de ma Vie* are particularly instructive, showing, as they do, the nature of the influence to which this strangely divided existence was subjected from its first conscious moment. Curiously enough, it was Madame de Genlis, the friend and instructress of kings, who in her *Battuécas*, a romance of innocent socialism (though this word had not yet been uttered), revealed to the thoughtful child many of the ideas which influenced her life—ideas which she always maintained with an ingenuousness unmodified by advancing years, and unaltered by the later studies and opinions which more than once impelled it to rather extravagant though perfectly sincere expression.

Her imagination worked actively and ceaselessly, though silently. She has said that she could trace its action in the earliest days of her childhood—that the life of the imagination formed the whole of her child-life. She distinctly remembered the moment of her first doubt on the existence of Father Christmas, the wonderful present-giver. This was a real grief. A child's first day of doubt is its last of careless happiness. "To suppress the marvellous in the life of a child is to set at naught the laws of nature. A child lives quite naturally in what are really supernatural conditions; for all within him is wonderful, and all without must at first sight appear wonderful also." Is not childhood itself, in its nearness to life's beginning, and in the flood of sensations which bring to it tidings of a new world, a perpetual series of marvels? George Sand takes every opportunity of joining issue with Rousseau in his notion that the marvellous should be suppressed because of its illusiveness. Nature understands her work: let her take her own time, and do not forestall anything. "No benefit can result from carelessly and thoughtlessly hastening a child's comprehension of all that strikes him. It is good that he should seek understanding for himself and in his own way at this period of his life, when our explanations, which he cannot understand, though they may dissipate his innocent mistakes, throw him into error both grave in itself and perhaps permanently injurious to the justness of his judgment, and therefore to the purity of his soul."

George Sand's was a dreamy nature. Even as a little child she would lose in endless reverie all sense of the world around her; and this habit of dreaming, which even in later life she found almost impossible to overcome, soon gave her a *stupid* look (*l'air bête*). "I say the word without hesitation, because throughout my life—in childhood, at the convent, and in the familiar intercourse of family life—it has always been applied to me, and therefore must be true." These visions were sometimes of an extreme and protracted intensity—such as that, for instance, into which she fell when her father died (she was then four years old); and as the meaning of death gradually dawned upon her she became speechless and sat for hours on a stool at her mother's feet, with drooping arms, fixed eyes, and half-opened mouth. "I have often seen her like this," said her mother to reassure the anxious family, "and it is natural to her; it is not stupidity; we may be sure that she is pondering over something." Indeed, this pondering or rumination was a constant habit of the already active mind. George Sand has vividly described this first and exclusively interior action of her imagination. She would never voluntarily read at this period of her life, as she was naturally idle, and delighted in idleness;—she tells us that only by the most strenuous efforts did she succeed in overcoming her idleness. The knowledge gained by eye and ear entered tumultuously into her little brain, and she would think about it all until she often lost, in her absorption, all sense of reality and of her actual surroundings. In such a nature one would expect to find the love of romance very strongly developed. She felt its power when still unconscious of its meaning, composing interminable stories, and acting them with her sister Caroline and her little companion Ursule. A strange medley were these! all that the small brain contained—a confusion of mythology and religion, resulting from the singular education which she received from her mother (an artist and poet in her way), "who would speak to her of the three Graces or the nine Muses as seriously as of the theological virtues or the wise virgins,"—and who would amalgamate the tales of Perrault and the fairy pieces of the boulevard "in such wise that angels and cupids, the wise virgin and the good fairy, Punch and the magicians, the imps of the theatre and the saints of the Church, produced in her mind the oddest poetical jumble that could be imagined."

This fermentation of ideas, so fantastically pictured in her mind and more distinctly represented in her games, subsided but did not cease when she went from the rooms in the Rue Grange-Batelière, which she and her mother occupied in Paris, to the house at Nohant, which belonged to Madame Dupin. Here quite another life awaited her—a life providing very different food for thought or *rumination.* After the lesson-hours, to which she was but outwardly attentive, she would spend her time with the little peasants of the neighbourhood in the pastures where they gathered round their fire—playing, dancing, or telling each other terrible stories, which she found inspiriting as she enjoyed their fears. "It is impossible for anyone to imagine," she has said in recalling these days of her childhood, "what takes place in the minds of children who live, as it were, with Nature, without in the least understanding her, and who have the strange faculty of seeing all that their imagination presents to them with their bodily eyes." She earnestly tried to share the hallucination peculiar to these country-folk—watching for the apparition of some grotesque animal, the passing of the *great beast* (*la grand' bête*), which nearly all her companions had seen at least once. She always took the chief part in the evening tales which went round when the hemp-dressers came to the farm. Notwithstanding her good-will, she says that she never succeeded in calling up a vision or in imposing upon herself; but the disturbance of nerves and imagination resulting from these attempts produced a kind of shivering pleasure, which she often tried to revive for the sake of the enjoyment that such excitement gave her. This was the only effect which she experienced from these rustic legends so eagerly collected and the night visions so assiduously courted: they merely thrilled her for a moment, robbing her perhaps of a few hours of sleep. But she was meanwhile amassing materials in her storehouse of fancy, and in incessant reverie preparing them for the future work of which she had as yet no thought: already an artist, she divided herself in two, as is the artist's wont—at once the author of and actor in the little dramas continually enacted in her mind. Later on she produced many studies in this kind of literature—the literature of fear which she had herself put to the test :—the *Diable aux Champs*, the *Contes d'une Grand'mère*, the *Légendes Rustiques*, the *Drac*, etc., etc. ; and thus acquired a wide and curious knowledge of the subject which interested her greatly, though her enjoyment was not unmixed with fear. The element of fancy was, in her opinion, a source of strength to the peasant mind, and she was especially pleased to discover its presence in races whose only relief in the rude miseries of material life lies in the power of imagination. The *Kobold* in Sweden, the *Korigan* in Brittany, the *Follet* in Berry, the *Orco* in Venice, the *Drac* in Provence,—there are few of her novels of adventure which do not contain some allusion to these creatures of popular legend, some touch of this lore-memories of her childhood's dreams.

Such was the prelude to the golden-age vision, the mirage of rural innocence which haunted the child and followed her even into mature life. Notwithstanding her rather melancholy preoccupations, she was not sad—she had her moments of frank, exuberant gaiety ; her life in childhood and youth seems to have been an alternation of contemplative solitude and wild excitement. On emerging from her interminable reveries, she would abandon herself in a kind of intoxication to the simplest and most active amusements, thus showing the strangest contradiction in the eyes of those around her. These "were the two aspects of a mind at once prone to melancholy and eager for gladness, perhaps the two aspects of a soul which could not rest satisfied with what interests the generality of men, yet was readily charmed with what appears to them puerile and illusory . . . . I cannot (she says) explain my nature more clearly. Judging from these contrasts, many people concluded that I was altogether odd."

The current of this interior and secret life which she already felt so vivid and intense within her, was nearly forced into an entirely different direction by the sufficiently grave experience of a religious crisis through which she passed in her sixteenth year. After a time of terrible and perpetually renewed heart-struggles, and on receiving some cruelly mistimed disclosures on her mother's past life, Aurore had resolved to renounce all which might in the future still more widely separate her mother and herself, who, even then, generally lived apart: she wished to renounce her grandmother's fortune, to cast away all instruction, all polish of manner, everything, in short, which might be called the world. She conceived a perfect horror for the lessons of her pedagogue, Deschartres, whose features, vanities, ridicules, and rough honesty she immortalised later on; she rebelled, and showed herself totally unmanageable.

Madame Dupin, not being able to subdue Aurore's mutiny, decided to place her in the English convent, which was at that time the favourite educational establishment in Paris for girls of the upper classes. To the young boarder, who arrived there nearly heart-broken by the last struggle between her mother and her grand-mother—the two beings most dear to her—this was a very haven of rest. Her account in the *Histoire de ma Vie* of her sojourn at the convent is exquisitely charming. She enlivens her story with some life-like portraits of the sisters and boarders, describes the manners and customs, the studies and the other rooms, and interests us in the various little dramas of the religious life,—in the pupils' quarrels and their reconciliations; their faults and the punishments incurred or undergone; the idle sauntering in the corridors and underground passages and on the roof of the convent; the search for a secret which had never existed, and for imaginary victims who —although even their names were unknown—were to be delivered from a romantic captivity. He we see already in action the conception wrought out in many of her novels, a conception which seems to haunt her incessantly,—the mysteries of *la Daniella*, *la Comtesse de Rudolstadt*, the *Château des Désertes*, *Flamarande*, and so many other works in which the plot is complicated by material surprises—labyrinths and mazes of fantastic architecture; and one feels as if one had discovered a secret collaboration of Anne Radcliffe with a writer of genius. George Sand has certain fixed ideas, and this one declared itself betimes.

In this company of extremely undisciplined girls, among whom she speedily found a place—sometimes following and sometimes leading them—her spirit, which had been temporarily quelled, revived in superabundant measure, and she joined the *demons*—a name which distinguished the girls who declined to be numbered either among the *studious* or the *dunces.* But after two years of very irregular and restless study, having exhausted the amusements which had nothing diabolic about them except the name—consisting merely in purposeless excitement and mute rebellion against rule,—a revolution suddenly took place in her mind. "It broke forth in a moment like a passion kindled in a soul ignorant of its own strength. . . . . A day arrived when her deep and tranquil love for Mother Alicia was no longer sufficient for her . . . . All her needs were of the heart, and her heart was wearied . . . ." An intense impulsion, like a special manifestation of the heavenly grace, transformed her. And one day, as in a dark corner of the chapel she was prostrate in meditation, she too heard the *Tolle, lege* of St. Augustine, which a picture before her naïvely represented. Without reservation or discussion she yields at once and wholly to the faith that besieges her soul—hers was no lukewarm nature, and she makes a point of honour of this utter self-abandonment. She suffered "the sacred melody" to its end—she gave herself up to devotion—she knew the burning tears of piety, the exaltations of faith, and she knew also its weariness and languor. Beneath the arches of the cloister the mystic fever excited her to a holy frenzy; kneeling till she was exhausted on the pavement of the chapel where the revelation had been made to her, she would sob out her very soul. Later on, she embodied her remembrances of this period of her life in her *Spiridion*, a narrative which glows with divine love in its earlier pages at least—for the tenderly enthusiastic soul of the young monk afterwards falls a prey to agitations and visions of another kind, which cause him to stray from his simple faith into new paths. But the beginning of the novel bears the impress of a deep and sincere religious emotion, and in no part of the author's life is this to be found in the same degree as in the sojourn at the English convent. The experience of the young monk Spiridion is her experience—life soon disturbed the beautiful mystic dream, dashed the ecstasy, and introduced new elements which profoundly modified the impression received; but she retained a germ of Christian idealism, which neither the accidents of life nor even her adventures could ever destroy: for though it might be temporarily crushed, it always revived.

The religious fever subsided on her return to Nohant, and the precarious state of health in which she found her grandmother (by whose rather anxious desire she had been recalled), and the painful suspense which it caused, obliged her once more to face the cares of practical life. During the last ten months of the slow and inevitable decay of this dear life, Aurore's days were spent at the bedside of Madame Dupin, or alone in sadness that seemed almost wild. This deep melancholy was only interrupted by "the reverie of the gallop," the rides which, without any special destination in view, took her through a rapidly varying scenery, now desolate, now lovely, and of which the only incidents noted in the reminiscences are some picturesque meeting with straying cattle or sheep, a flight of birds, the sound of a plashing brook beneath the horse's feet, or the breakfast at a farm with her little rustic page André, trained by Deschartres not to disturb the dreamy silence. It was then that the spirit of poetry, stirred by her intense feeling of outward things, awoke within her; but she did not know it or perceive it.

It was at this time also, that, becoming conscious of the blank left in her mind by the fragmentary and hap-hazard education which she had received, first under Deschartres' very peculiar discipline, and afterwards under the too indulgent convent-rule, she resolved to begin a course of self-instruction. She threw herself eagerly into studies of which she grew passionately fond, reading enormously, but with tumultuous curiosity, without aim and without method. And now another change took place in her mind. She laid aside the *Imitation of Christ* and the doctrine of humility, for the *Génie du Christianisme*, though this book served rather as an introduction to romantic poetry than to a new form of religious truth. She soon turned to the study of philosophy: every new book seemed to mark a fresh era in her life. There is nothing, in my opinion, more dangerous to an ardent and inexperienced mind than strong and indiscriminate doses of metaphysics. For a young understanding is exposed to this twofold peril: it either attaches itself exclusively, and with the exclusive enthusiasm of a sectary, to a single doctrine, while yet incapable of examining it impartially; or it confounds and intermixes all doctrines in an ill-judging eclecticism, and attempts to reconcile, by affinities of thought, discrepant names and doctrines, such as those of Christ and Spinoza. This youthful dreamer did not escape these errors; she wavered between the enthusiasm which confounds all doctrines, and that which attaches itself exclusively to a single doctrine or a single name, as the feeling of the moment or the caprice of imagination directed. But she rapidly increased her capital of knowledge, which, though badly enough distributed, soon became considerable. Without the least hesitation, she had entered the lists with Mably, Locke, Condillac, Montesquieu, Bacon, Bossuet, Aristotle, Leibnitz—whom, as metaphysician, she ranked above all the rest (a happy distinction and preference),—Montaigne, and Pascal. Then came the poets and moralists,—La Bruyère, Pope, Milton, Dante, Virgil, Shakespeare: all without the least idea of connexion or order of study—she took them just as they fell in her way. The whirling confusion of ideas thus engendered was mastered with singular and intuitive facility; the brain was deep and wide, the memory docile, the feeling true and rapid, the will on the stretch. At last Rousseau arrived. She recognised her master, yielded to the imperious charm of his fervid logic, and her divorce from Catholicism was consummated.

Her nervous force had exhausted itself in this conflict of opinions and doctrines, in the effort to comprehend, to reconcile or to choose. Châteaubriand's *René*, *Hamlet*, and above all Byron, put the final touch to the work; she fell into a state of utter intellectual and moral disorder, and was seized with a melancholy which she did not even try to resist. She resolved to detach herself as much as possible from life, and presently the disgust of life produced the desire of death. She never approached the river without saying to herself, with a kind of feverish pleasure, "How easy it is! I should only have to make one step!" Yes or no? She repeated this often enough to have risked being plunged by the *yes* into the transparent water which attracted her so powerfully. One day the *yes* was said; she urged her horse out of the fordable crossing into the deep water beyond. It would have been all over with her and her future masterpieces if the good mare Collette had not saved her by an extraordinary leap out of the dangerous depths.

The death of her grandmother, whose last moments she describes with unaffected grief and touching truth, closes the initiatory period. The division between her paternal and maternal kindred was completed by the opening of the will. Her mother had long been aware of the clause which separated her from her daughter; she was also aware of the importance attached to that clause. Hence arose fresh disturbances. Certain concessions were made. Aurore was obliged to break with her Villeneuve relations, to whose care she had been commended by the wish of her dead grandmother, and this caused another family disruption.

To relieve this strained and at times intolerable situation, Madame Dupin took her daughter into the country, to some friends whom she had met three days before—the Duplessis—who proved the best friends imaginable; they lived with their children in a beautiful villa of La Brie. She promised that she would come for Aurore "next week": she left her there five months; and there, one day, the marriage which was to put a natural end to the stormy and sometimes ridiculous family relations, and give the young girl some hope of a peaceful existence, took place.

Here again illusion was not wanting. Aurore was reputed to be an heiress of considerable beauty and lively disposition, when not exposed to her mother's fits of passion and irritability, which were wont to make her intensely melancholy. It was under the Duplessis' roof that she met M. Dudevant, who was the illegitimate son of a retired colonel, and possessed a fortune equal to her own. He immediately took a fancy to her, "although he did not speak to her of love, confessing indeed that he was not prone to sudden passion or enthusiasm, and that he was certainly unskilled in expressing those feelings in an attractive manner." Aurore was once, in jest, treated as his future wife. This was all that was needed: she allowed herself to be married almost passively, as passively as she performed all the outward actions of her life. The marriage took place in the September of 1822; they went to Nohant, where her chief occupation during the winter of 1823 was the anticipation of the motherhood which was drawing near, amid the fairest dreams and most fervent aspirations. She was completely transformed. The needs of the intellect, the restlessness of thought, the curiosities of study and of observation, all disappeared, she says, as soon as the sweet burden was felt. "Providence wills that in this phase of hope and waiting the physical life and the life of feeling should predominate. Therefore the watches, the studies, the dreams—the intellectual life, in a word, was naturally suppressed, and that without the least merit or the least regret." Her husband was of a negative and interfering disposition; his life was spent in hunting. She, utterly without support or help at hand, forebore to dream, and made her preparations with an eagerness, and before long a *maestria* in the fashioning of her work, that surprised herself.

If we except the episode of motherhood, this new life opened drearily enough. It was only by accident, and much later, that the crises of painful exaltation which until then had been her secret torment, and what is more dangerous, her secret and cherished delight, returned. Some years passed in a kind of prosaic tranquillity and negative happiness. Two beautiful children were beside her: her dreams seemed very far away. If we may believe her, she had become to al appearance a "stolid countrywoman" (*une campagnarde engourdie*), and she was even intent on becoming a good housekeeper,—a more difficult matter. But if her thoughts still worked solitarily in the very homely conditions of life to which she seemed to be condemned, the young mother did not parade her mental agitations: no one about her knew of them or even suspected their existence; and when her first novels had been produced, one of her dearest friends, le Malgache, who had been a frequent guest at Nohant, wrote: "*Lélia* is a fancy. There is no likeness to you here—to you who are lively, who dance the *bourrée*, who appreciate the *lepidoptera*, who do not despise puns, do not sew badly, and make preserves very well." When (towards 1831) her home-life became seriously troubled; when her schemes for a future according to her liking had prevailed; when a miserable allowance and her liberty had been vouchsafed to her (a legal separation in her favour was afterwards obtained); when she arrived in Paris, there to run the fearful risk of a wholly emancipated life,—it was then that Madame Sand became known: a different woman and a different name. Henri Delatouche gave her that name. *Sand* was the joint property of Jules Sandeau and herself, who were associated in a collaboration for the first work. The Christian names were speedily agreed upon: Sandeau kept his own, and George was the synonym of *Berrichon*, the characteristic name of a native of Berry. "Jules and George, who are unknown to the public, might pass for brothers or cousins." The two names soon gained a celebrity that placed an increasing distance between them.

We are not relating a biography: we merely attempt a psychological sketch; our design was to note the various trials and intellectual phases of Madame Sand's youth. She began her literary life with a very real experience of suffering, though it had doubtless been exaggerated by a strong imagination, vivid emotions, and religious agitations; she had been rather irritated than soothed by her ill-regulated studies; was acutely and delicately sensitive, and profoundly disdainful of the relative truths which must, at times, perforce content us as the world goes; she had an instinctive hatred of every yoke imposed by law or opinion, and an innate horror of all that endangers the freedom of the mind or of the heart. Add to this that, by the miracle of a lavish nature, she found herself almost at her first attempt in possession of a marvellous style, which seems to have been created for the purpose of expressing her ardent thought, formed alone and without aid from the time of the long series of little note-books dedicated to the epopee of *Corambé* to that in which her first work was given to the public.

Whence came the first revelation of her literary talent? This is a matter of interest to us. It seems to have shown itself towards the end of the last autumn at Nohant; she had been extensively reading Scott, whose influence may be recognised in many of her novels.

During her long walks in these sad months she worked out the idea of a species of romance, which was never to see the light, and which she wrote on the shelf of an old cupboard or press in her grandmother's boudoir, with her children by her side. "Having read it," she candidly says, "I was convinced that it was worthless, but that I might do less badly"; and being then absorbed in choosing an occupation that would secure her liberty in Paris, she began to think that it was no worse than many others which more or less supply the means of subsistence. "I perceived that I could write quickly, easily, and for a long time without fatigue; that my ideas, benumbed in my brain, awoke and connected themselve by deduction, at the movement of the pen; that in my life of contemplation I had observed much and had fairly well understood the characters which chance had brought before me, and that I therefore understood human nature sufficiently well to portray it." This encouraged her in her attempt, and led her to conclude that of all the small employments of which she was capable, that of literature, properly so called, for which she had a confused taste and instinct, offered her as a profession the best chance of success. So she made her choice. But there had been much previous hesitation. She had occasionally tried her skill in portraiture in crayon or water-colour; but though her likenesses were faithful, it seems that they lacked originality. Once she thought that she had certainly discovered her real aptitude, for she painted ornamental birds and flowers and microscopic compositions on snuff-boxes and cigar-cases of Spa-wood with considerable taste, and she nearly sold one of these, through a dealer to whom she had entrusted it, for eighty francs. Literary destinies verily turn upon slight causes! Had it sold for a hundred francs—the price which she fearfully asked, without believing she should get it,—*Consuelo* and *La Mare au Diable* would never have appeared. Happily, the fashion for these trifles soon passed, and Madame Dudevant was obliged to look elsewhere for a means of gaining her bread—for her *gagne-pain.* The word is her own, and the conditions forced upon her made it strictly correct. When from pure weariness, and to buy her independence, she had yielded all her rights to her husband, it became clear that she must win her way through the life of freedom by her own labour. This husband (whom we shall not again encounter on our way), though he had not been exactly an *offensive reality* in the earlier years, and though he was not as a rule unkind or brutal, had contrived both to make himself unbearable, and the common life very difficult to a woman whose tastes and habits could neither be modified nor subdued. It seems that other and graver faults added to the conjugal difficulties, and determined the separation, which was at first partial and freely allowed, but afterwards became decisive.

The time came when Madame Dudevant regained her full right to the independence which she had so often desired, for in 1836 the Court of Justice at Bourges decreed the separation in her favour, and gave her the custody of the two children. But she had then already made the dangerous experiment of literary celebrity by works that had compelled the public attention. She had gained it by qualities which we know had been put to the test in her life of retirement—a retirement inwardly so troubled: the long day-dreams in which she sought a refuge from the real life, a very keen sensibility to every form of human suffering, a goodness which was at once a source of inspiration and a perpetual cause of error and misunderstanding in her life, and lastly an inexhaustible imagination, of which she had delightedly followed the alternately entrancing and terrible combinations, until the day when she conceived the idea of giving them to the public. They were received with intense enthusiasm, and the name of the enchantress was greeted with a chorus of applause. A place was soon granted her—and it was often the first place—in the illustrious pleiad of novelists, which included the very different names of Balzac, Alexandre Dumas, and Jules Sandeau; and the name of George Sand shone therein with its own particular brightness, borrowing no light from the brother-stars.

CHAPTER II.

THE HISTORY OF GEORGE SAND'S WORKS.—THE ORDER AND PSYCHOLOGICAL SUCCESSION OF HER NOVELS.

WHAT was George Sand's idea of the novel when she began to write for the public? Even in allowing the widest scope to the action of spontaneity, is it possible that such a richly endowed and fertile intellect should have followed any course that suggested itself at random, with the vulgar indifference of a mind that cares only to succeed? Was it not rather developed by the unperceived but active rule of vigorous and permanent instincts? She will answer us herself:

"I had no theory whatever when I began to write, and I do not think that I ever had one when the desire to write a novel impelled me to take pen in hand. This does not alter the fact that my instincts formed, unconsciously to myself, the theory which I am about to advance, that which I have generally followed without knowing that I did so, that which is, even as I write, still under discussion. According to this theory, the novel should be as much a poetical as an analytical work. It requires true and even real situations and characters, grouped about a type intended to show forth the feeling or the principal idea of the book. This type generally represents the passion of love, since nearly all novels are histories of love. According to the theory enunciated (and it is here that it begins), this love (consequently this type) must be idealised, and one must not fear to endow it with all the powers to which one aspires oneself, or with all the sorrows of which one has seen or felt the wounds. But in no case must it be depreciated by the accident of circumstances; it must either die or triumph; and one must not fear to give it an importance which is exceptional in life, a might above the common, and charms or sufferings far beyond the usual level of human things, even exceeding the limits of the *probable* as understood by the generality of minds. To recapitulate: the idealisation of the feeling which constitutes the subject, leaving to the art of the narrator the care of placing that subject in conditions and in a setting sufficiently real to show it off."

George Sand was not infallible in her application of this theory: her idealisation is in more than one instance chimerical and false. But there her judgment erred, not her instinct; she was faithful in intention to her theory even when she belied it. And her theory seems very grand and simple, especially if we compare it with what appeared later.

Through all the adventures of her real and literary life George Sand remained true to her worship of the ideal, true to her poet-nature; the changing taste of later generations can never deprive her of this honour. Her rich and varied works are born of a poetical conception; they often deteriorate in the course of development, but the beginning is always marvellous.

One can understand how this spontaneity of the imagination, which I have tried to trace to its troubled sources, an imagination which does not control but rather excites itself—how the remembrance of the moral crises passed through, the confused hope of a future in which her own enthusiastic credulity saw the fruition of divine dreams—how all this restless, quivering, proud nature, with its illusions and its real sorrows, will instinctively find expression in works strange and bold in conception, fervid and disquieting in style, full of pain and passion, overflowing with lyricism touching love, religion, and human life. And further, if one reflects that this author is a woman who has been wounded by her contact with life and deceived and irritated in a thousand ways, that by her very lonely and retired, though inwardly most active existence, she has been cut off from the view of all the stirring scenes of the political and social world, and that she throws herself into this unknown in her absolute inexperience, with her illimitable desires, a deep compassion for all the human pain and misery that cries aloud for help, and a profounder pity for that which bleeds and suffers in silence,—if one reflects upon all this, one will understand how this woman was appalled and startled at the sight, as are all the beautiful souls who judge the world by their heart, and whose aspirations are mercilessly crushed by the brutality of facts. She will ask, then, if there is no remedy for all these evils.

At first, her mind and her works will be dominated by personal religious and moral preoccupations. Presently social preoccupations will prevail. And then around this inspired woman, this applauded poet, this already popular writer, will throng the doctors of the Universal Renovation, the empirics and the Utopists, the sophists and the dreamers, the sincere and the quack-doctors, apostles of the social question, the impostors and the dupes, the ambitious and the simple. In George Sand they have found a brilliant herald of their doctrine. They outvie each other in propounding to her for vulgarisation new plans and unpublished systems—the philosophy, the politics, the religion of the future. George Sand's nature predisposed her to submit to the despotism of stern convictions and strong imaginations. A fanatical worshipper of absolute good, or, failing that, of an immediately attainable improvement (rather dreamed of than practically tried), more indolent in conceiving the idea than in working it out, and knowing that she lacked the intellectual initiative power, she allows a considerable period of her life to be absorbed in political Utopianism, in the vague longing for a golden age on the advent of which all around her agree, while no one will resign his particular plan for hastening its coming, or his special programme for realising it. But at last will dawn a happy day (yes, it was a happy day for her talent and her glory) when she will become profoundly weary of this agitation of ideas in space, of these theories which are immaculate and superb only so long as they remain upon the interior throne of pure thought, becoming *degraded and polluted by events* as soon as they descend into the arena of active politics and into the movements of the streets. This great spirit, which has a horror of violence, will retire into itself under the influence of fatigue and disgust; George Sand will, if I may so speak, make a spiritual retreat in the sanctuary of her dearest memories; she will yield to the energetic appeal of the secret instincts which have been too long wounded by violent discussion and unprofitable strife; she will return to her delight in the country, to her love for the fields of Berry, the scene of the early poetry of her childish dreams; and there will be in her a sudden and unhoped-for blossoming of fresh and charming remembrances, of pure and exquisite emotions. So at last we shall rest with her from all the agitations and all the hatreds, and the soft veiled light of the native country will eclipse and extinguish the feverish brightness of the reformer, the fiery dream of the *humanitarian* poet.

Is not this just the circle travelled round by Madame Sand, and is not this page from the biography of her inner life an epitomised history of her works?

I.

The first division of her literary life is a period of spontaneous and subjective lyricism. And as I wish here to give a classification which shall not be arbitrary, but historical and as relatively exact as is possible in an entirely psychological arrangement, I think we may consider that this first period extends from 1832 to about 1840. During this interval of nine years the masterpieces of the first manner appeared in close succession: *Indiana*, *Valentine*, *Jacques*, *André*, *Mauprat*, *Lélia*, and the charming series of Venetian stories.*

Let us briefly recall the subjects of the principal works. We shall see that they all have a common origin in personal emotions and sorrows, though they must not be considered as a faithful picture and record of her life. Madame Sand always protested against the too strictly biographical interpretations that were applied to her earlier novels.

Still we must come to a clear understanding on this delicate point. *Indiana* is not, she assures us, her unveiled history, but it is, nevertheless, the expression of her habitual reflexions, of her moral agitations, of a part of her real or fictitious sufferings. It is not her life, I grant, but it is the romance or the drama of her life, such as she conceived it beneath the shades of Nohant. And though it is not—and I believe this—a formulated

* These are the dates of the principal novels :—In 1832, *Indiana* and *Valentine;* in 1833, *Lélia;* in 1834, the *Lettres d'un Voyageur* and *Jacques;* in 1835, *André* and *Léone Léoni;* from 1833-1838, the *Secrétaire Intime*, *Lavinia*, *Metella*, *Mattea*, *la Dernière Aldini*. *Mauprat* was written at Nohant in 1836, when Madame was petitioning for a separation. Such chronological references throw light upon the author's thought.

plaint against her particular master, it is at least a protestation against tyranny in married life, personified by Colonel Delmare. It was also the conception, the ideal of the loving woman as she then imagined her; it was on her own account that she interested herself in the portraiture of a love deep and simple, exalted and sincere, passionate and chaste,—a love which is betrayed by its very simplicity, which in its sincerity falls a prey, with no defence save chance, to the voluptuous and ruthless selfishness of a man of the world, and which is at last saved from utter despair by an heroically silent heart, a heart worthy of it, worthy to reconcile it with life and friendship. *Valentine* reproduces, with exquisite details and incomparable poetry, this theme of the sacrilegious and unhappy marriage enjoined by worldly expedience, a marriage which brings in its train the most grievous and tragical sorrows, the violent awakening of nature and of the heart, fatal passions, temptation stronger than the will, a family dishonoured, a noble house disgraced, a home made desolate. In *Jacques* we have her ideal of love in man (as in *Indiana* we have her ideal of love in woman), a Stoic succumbing to love, and loving with the depth and loftiness which a Stoic can bring to such matter. A spirit sad even unto death when it foresees a weakness or a betrayal; a self-devoted lover who quietly yields up all his right, and resigns himself to suicide, that Fernande may be spared the humiliation of a guilty joy and the shame of a dishonoured happiness. Love in a weak and gentle nature, which it exalts and crushes; love again, but in an untamed nature, which it conquers, raising heart and understanding to the highest point of development,—these are studies on the different effects of the grand passion;—this is *André*, this is *Mauprat*. *Lélia!* who having read can ever forget this poem, so strange, incoherent, magnificent, and absurd, where spirituality falls so low, where sensuality aspires so high; where despair declaims in such wondrous style; where the spirit, entranced, startled, scandalised, passes swiftly from a scene of debauch to sublime prayer; where the most fantastic inspiration flashes from the lowest depths to heaven itself, only to fall again and sink to yet deeper depths! Here are doubt, which curses, which blasphemes, which melts in ecstasy; love, which reviles itself without pity, and analyses its misery in a kind of despairing fury; faith, which now abjures itself, now loses itself in rapture; the ideal, which is dragged down to foulest degradation, and seeks in its orgies a vain consolation for its disappointed dreams and aspirations. This excessive lyricism, though out of date, still presents to the reader an amazing spectacle, in which frenzy and delirium are mingled with flights of the greatest beauty. In *Spiridion*, the young monk Alexis (who bears a considerable resemblance to George Sand herself in consultation with Lammenais) represents the soul, bewildered in the quest of religious truth, touched by the divine ideal, and with painful anxiety seeking it in symbols, in books, and above all in the agony of an aged dying monk, who bequeaths to his successor the flame which was taken from the fire of the storm, the flame which will kindle a religious revolt, and, later on, the Revolution.

In viewing these great novels we must not forget the lesser works—less in extent, that is, but not in talent. They who do not know Madame Sand's smaller stories do not really know her; they are, at least, unlikely to be able to appreciate the wonderful flexibility of her art. In all her greater works, in all the different periods of her life, though chiefly in the first, a dancing, sparkling current of pure French humour plays at intervals—a revival of the humour of the eighteenth century, elegant in fancy, adventurous in curiosity, flowing in joyous freedom through all the romances where the theme, perpetually varied, is love. Has the delicacy of irony ever been treated more gracefully than by the hand that wrote *Cora* and *Lavinia*—traced the pages in which the last *marquise* of the eighteenth century, while she is playing with her fan, describes to us the manners and characters of her day, and tells us of the one emotion that almost troubled the tranquil current of a long life given to idle loves? And *Lavinia*—who could forget her? Long after she has disappeared, the impression of that smile lingers with us, that smile which betrays the malign vengeance of a deceived heart, that sees the return of the fugitive, and, with smiling melancholy, leaves him, in its turn, to a remorse which is speedily consoled. In all these tales how natural is the invention, how lively the manner, how exquisite the tone and the style! *Metella* shows us both vividly and naturally the art of delineating the deepest sorrows of the heart, with the reserved touch that allows all to be divined, though it indicates scarcely anything, merely glancing over the surface. The *Secrétaire Intime* and *Teverino* are two most brilliantly poetical creations.

I like *Léone Léoni* less, despite its extraordinary vigour of style; and there are some pages in *la Dernière Aldini* that are not much to my taste. The mother pleases me but indifferently when she wishes to marry her gondolier, and the daughter frightens me when she throws herself at the singer. But how many other pages full of freshness and brilliancy, and what radiant colouring! what subtlety and grace in the scene where Lelio finds himself, for the first time, alone with the young Alezia! What an ingenious contest! and then the charming triumph for both! The splendour of George Sand's great works has been so dazzling, and they have been panegyrised and discussed so ardently, that the novelettes have in some degree suffered. Yet among them are to be found some of the purest gems of this overflowing casket—all the charms of the mind unite to furnish a golden setting for some delicate thought. A tender grace, a smiling fancy, an originality now pungent, now touching—how many enchanting gifts! how one regrets that George Sand was not satisfied with them! why did she make of her talent a more powerful but often discordant instrument for the interpretation of doctrines which she but imperfectly understood?

With these tales—of which the form and the scenery

are Italian, and especially Venetian—should be compared the *Lettres d'un Voyageur*, published at different times and at considerable intervals; the earlier ones, the Venetian letters, possessing a singular and most vivid interest which we do not find to the same degree in the others. These first letters, a very prose-poem—a chronicle of wanderings in the Alps and in the neighbourhood of the Tyrol; also an account of conversations and solitary impressions at Venice—are the sorrowful and dramatic expression of a suffering, drooping spirit, already cruelly tried by grief and deceived by love, as if, after but a few years of experience, it had been constrained to a self-demonstration of the truth that the most romantic passions are not exempt from suffering, any more than are the most commonplace existences. There is now a bitterly resigned judgment on life and on mankind, now a sharp plaint, a cry of anguish, such a cry as is heard throughout the world and long re-echoes. It is assuredly the most touching and most curious revelation of herself that Madame Sand has made in the sincerity of the tone and the exquisite reserve of grief. In these simple pages we see a single soul agitated by all the most sacred feelings of the soul; they are tossed, they palpitate beneath the veil—neither the age nor the sex of this poor, poetic traveller of life is discovered for an instant. Passion and suffering preserve an admirable delicacy, and this redoubles the charm.

All these works, while they differ greatly in conception, in fancy, and in form, bear the burning impress of a young mind. The subject, virtually the same amid a dazzling variety of adventure, is the representation of noble love in its battle with the temptations and surprises of life, the defections or deceptions; it is the fate of the poor, great human heart in its delusive flights of heroism and its immeasurable falls; it is also the struggle of loving souls against the treachery of fortune which delivers them to violence as its prey; it is the revolt of nature against the fatal errors of society; it is a protestation against the tyranny of law or opinion—in a word, against all which checks the impulses of true love. Finally, it is the anxious and passionate quest of the religious ideal, an ideal often chimerical and confused, but ardently longed for, and dimly perceived amid the lowering clouds of "superstition and scepticism." Such is the inspiration which reigns in the first period and ends the subject of the earlier songs. Each of these works is a poem dedicated to Divine love, and perhaps more especially to human love, each wondering at being so closely associated and confounded together. The social question only appears in the far distance and incidentally; at first her idea of reformation embraces little more than marriage, which is, indeed, criticised less in its principle than in its practical working. She wrote at this time, as she tells us, under the influence of an emotion, not of a system.

II.

The system soon appears, and the emotion is driven back and forced within strict bounds. The emotion and the system—one proceeding from the author's inmost soul, the other coming from without—more or less equally divide the novels of the second period, those which occupy Madame Sand's literary life from 1840 to about 1848.

This division was a misfortune from an artistic point of view. One cannot exactly say that there is evidence of declining talent in the works of the second manner, but the interest is certainly less sustained, and one's sympathy, which is constantly repulsed, becomes chilled. That this should happen was inevitable. What she promised us in the novel was the more or less idealised portraiture of the human heart, the analysis of the soul in fictitious situations, its development in this combination of imaginary events according to the pleasure of the author, observer, or poet: what pleased us in that study was the enjoyment of a delicious forgetfulness of the actual world, a rest from that feverish toil in which our treasure of feeling and activity becomes exhausted, by a necessary effect of practical life, in hard and ever-recurring struggles, of which the object is often so miserable. The relief from the strife, the noise, the dust of every day was delightful. O poet! thou didst lure me with the attraction of a lovely story; I followed thee confidingly, and my heart was charmed; thou didst entreat my interest, thou hast fascinated it; thou didst touch me, I feel the sweet intoxication of thy art. And suddenly my emotion is checked and chilled. What hast thou done? In the midst of the enchanting idyl behold a perfidious tirade, of which I recognise the inspirer, behold the beginning of the socialistic lecture! The charm has ceased to act. Thou dost thrust me back by main force and by a species of treachery into the region of discord and agitation from which I would fain have fled. I recognise here the speech of M. Michel (de Bourges), there the fiery pamphlet of M. de Lammenais, elsewhere the philosophic and religious dream of M. Pierre Leroux; hasten after my emotion, try to recover it, for it is very far distant. I will add that, by the mere force of things, the talent and style are no longer the same in these interludes of intermittent preaching. One distinctly feels that the inspiration is from without, and that these words are but an echo. Then comes the inevitable declamation, as it always does when the style is no longer the distinct sound of the soul directly struck by its own emotion. The eloquence becomes strained, the forced enthusiasm appears bombastic.

Let this criticism be tried on the principal novels of this second period. It is towards 1840, with the *Compagnon du Tour de France*, that the system appears, and that socialism takes the field. There are certainly charming scenes in this novel, there are types and situations artistically realised. The subject of the work is, or at least ought to be, the contrasting of the generous and truly great love of Pierre Huguenin with the vain and sensual passion of Amaury; one dedicating the ardour of his chaste feeling to a grave, austere maiden who is all intelligence and all soul, the other seeking the satisfaction of artistic taste in the dishonour of a woman of fashion, a coquette, whom he loves with all the pride of his senses and all the exultation of a fancy. What is true in this work, keenly observed and very fine, is the effect on Amaury of this false and evil love. This gifted but weak nature, which has been duped by its vanity, sorely expiates its fault, not by the loss of its future, but, what is more terrible, by the successive degradation of its noble qualities. Voluptuousness and ambition have touched it; they will for ever retain their hold. What is also true and admirably described is the effect of a noble love in Pierre Huguenin—the delineation of his moral elevation, of the delicate pride of his feeling, of the courage and uprightness, of the good-sense which keeps in the background and in the shade, where all impossible passions should be banished. But alas! these keen analyses are abruptly checked at every moment; this profound and charming study on the effect upon two plebeian spirits of two contrary passions is interrupted, that the torrent of political declamation may flow on.

I know no more troublesome, more noisy and more foolishly garrulous individual than the Achille Lefort whom one is certain to find at every turn of the path whenever the idyl takes the air. There can be nothing more improbable than the character of M. de Villepreux, the accomplice of Achille Lefort, whom he despises—an indefinable mixture of a sceptical nobleman, a member of the constitutional opposition, and a conspirator without convictions, who at certain moments seems to mount the tripod of the Humanitarian Sibyl, and the instant afterwards descends into the simile of a Machiavelli of the Palais-Bourbon. Above all, I can imagine nothing more false, more declamatory, and more discordant than the character of the noble Yseult, in the last part of the novel, where one is amazed to discover that the young girl, who seems to be the personification of reason, and is so graceful and charming, is merely a hot-headed conspirator and an infatuated pedant. See her initiating Pierre Huguenin into the mysteries of Carbonarism, and establishing the Lodge *Jean-Jacques Rousseau* in the midst of that magnificent scenery, in that beautiful park! Then having been in her turn enlightened on the true doctrine of equality by the workman's virtue, suddenly, in a strange scene, asking him, "before God who sees and hears them," if he loves her as she loves him, and confessing that from the time when she found herself capable of reasoning on the future she had resolved "to marry a man of the people, so that she might become one of the people," as those who were disposed towards Christianity sought baptism that they might call themselves Christians! Sweet and charming Yseult, where are you? I know not what phantom escaped from a woman's club has taken your place. I no longer recognise you.* Thus at every turn, to the great annoyance of the reader, the two elements of the novel cross each other: one so altogether sweet and charming, and imbued with that charm which is the grace of art; the other charged with harsh and glaring discords, at which that grace takes fright, and then it speedily flies.

Horace would have been an interesting analysis of a miserably weak and selfish character, if the novel had not been spoilt by a visibly forced contrast of the character of Arsène, the sublime representative of the people, the hero of the rising Socialism, the type of every virtue, according to the new morality. In *Jeanne* we see the dawning of the *Druidical idea* so dear to some of Madame Sand's friends, combined with an undefinable and vague synthesis, an inexpressible religious chaos. Here again one would exercise the power of choice on a heterogeneous work. A few charming episodes—such as the finding Jeanne asleep among the *Pierres Jomâtres*, and the April Fools' Day; a few admirably depicted rustic scenes—such as the fire in a hamlet, the *lavandières*, death in the country, hay-making—do not counterbalance the weariness caused by the preponderance of the system which incessantly obstructs the free course of feeling. Little by little the system destroys the novel. The time comes when Jeanne ceases to be a child of the

* The Russian novel has often shown us, in these later times, this type of a Nihilistic Yseult. In France the type is still fictitious.

fields, admirably simple and pure, with an artless charm that inspires friendship or love in all who come across her, and so delicately modest in her wonder or affright at this. She alters visibly. Presently she becomes the Velléda of Mont Barlot, then the *Grande Pastoure ;* she rises higher and higher—if, from an artistic point of view, to pass into the region of myth and allegory is to rise. She symbolises the heroic and dreamy spirit of the peasantry. Well, I do not object; but I shut the book directly the peasant-girl begins to talk so finely, and hastily turn to *Consuelo.*

Here again, notwithstanding the treasures of art and invention so freely lavished on this book, shall I find no cause for vexation in it? I have certainly not such a foolish anxiety to prove the truth of my criticism as to question the wonderful richness of imagination, the curious interest, and the passion which pervade the whole of this novel, and the first part of the *Comtesse de Rudolstadt*, which is the continuation of it. Madame Sand felt, as she tells us, that here were a grand subject and powerful character-types, and an epoch and countries strewn with historical episodes which in their inner aspect were full of interest to the explorer; her imagination wandered among them at pleasure and with ever-increasing emotion, continually thrilled and tempted onwards by new vistas. She was drawn to this singular and complex enterprise by some recent studies which had vividly impressed her mobile mind, making her perceive the interest attaching to the eighteenth century as regards art, philosophy, and the marvellous—three elements which that century produced in an apparently heterogeneous fashion. The finding of the link that connected them promised to be a matter of curious and not too fanciful consideration. Century of Maria Theresa and Frederick II, of Voltaire and Cagliostro; strange century that begins in song, proceeds in fantastic conspiracies, and ends through profound ideas in formidable revolutions! I willingly acknowledge, with Madame Sand, the grandeur of the subject; and being more generous towards her than she is towards herself, I also acknowledge that she has generally made the most of it by the interest of her plot, the singular charm of some of the situations, and the brilliant delineation of feeling and character. How lovable is that Consuelo of lofty intelligence, noble heart, and admirable artistic power in the chastely-daring outset of her wandering life at Venice; in her first triumphs and sadnesses; in her arrival, on a stormy night, at that terrible *Château des Géants*, amid a phantasmagoria of ancient ruins and deep vaults; in her love for the young Count Albert, which, in her terror, she so longs resists; in her flight, in her meeting in the fields with the young Haydn, and afterwards in the long journey—surely the most enchanting and fantastic journey that imagination ever conceived!

And later, when—at war with terrible circumstances, the sad betrothed of Death, the victim of a fearful mystery which at times disturbed her reason—Consuelo, still a great and noble artist, reappears as the Comtesse de Rudolstadt, a maiden widow, and we meet her at the court of Frederick in a dangerous intimacy with the Princess Amélie, how fascinating and startling are the scenes! Her imprisonment, her abduction, the new flight under the charge of the *Invisibles*, the painful emotions caused by an enigmatical passion which attracts her as a permitted love, and frightens her as an unfaithfulness towards the dead—all this is described with unrivalled spirit and charm. But, save me from Count Albert, with his fatalism, his prolixity, and his gloom! If he loves Consuelo, let him tell her so, instead of perpetually descanting—in an imaginative story—on the barbarous legends concerning John Ziska and the Hussites. If his madness were not so affected he might possibly interest us; if he did not present himself at every moment with his pale brow, his fixed eye, and his black mantle strewn with silvery drops like a pall, he might possibly be agreeable. But it is too bad of him to be constantly talking nonsense to frighten Consuelo and irritate the reader. And then, when the moment of initiation arrives, and the Oracle speaks, at last, in the depths of the vault—do I mistake, and is it the noble Count that I hear? I somehow fancy that I recognise certain well-worn phrases which have done long and valiant service in the *Démocratie Pacifique* of the time and elsewhere: "A mysterious and singular sect cherished the dream, among many others, of rehabilitating the life of the flesh, of reuniting, in one divine principle, these two principles which have been arbitrarily divided.

It desired to sanction love, *equality*, and the *universal communism*—the elements of happiness. It sought to raise the principle of evil from its state of abjection, making it, on the contrary, the servant and the agent of the principle of good . . ." etc., etc. The noble Count may continue indefinitely—I have been dreaming for some time, and I suspect that Consuelo's great patience in listening to him is explained by the fact that she is following my example. But this is nothing compared to the second volume of the *Comtesse de Rudolstadt.* Here, anyone of great courage may with advantage view the rising tide of system and declamation. The tedium suddenly increases inordinately. Who could resolve to follow Consuelo into the grotesque Pantheon opened to her by the priests and priestesses of Truth, where, between the pillars, are statues of the greatest benefactors of humanity—Christ appearing between Pythagoras and Plato, Apollonius of Tyana beside St. John, Abelard near St. Bernard, John Huss and Jerome of Prague beside St. Catherine and Joan of Arc? Pray let us pause on the threshold of the Temple before Spartacus arrives to close the story, before all the characters of the novel in whom we have taken more or less interest disappear in a cloud of universal symbolism. Another novel which culminates in what is above all things most dreary—Allegory, and what is above all things most pompously empty—Humanitarian Theosophy.

It would really be an abuse of evidence were I to

insist further and repeat at length the same tedious experiment on *le Meunier d'Angibault*, at the beginning of which an heroic artisan, the great Lémor, refuses the hand of a rich widow whom he adores, because to be rich is against his principles, and at the end the rich widow is made to rejoice in the fire which destroys her château, because in the fall of the last bit of wall that belongs to her she sees the fall of the last obstacle that divides her from Socialism and her lover. Shall we mention the *Péché de M. Antoine?*—his greatest sin does not, to my thinking, consist in his having such a pretty daughter as Gilberte, but rather in his having made of M. de Boisguilbault the most insupportable of men by taking away his wife. Everyone is more or less communistic in the singular world to which the characters of the novel belong—M. Antoine, the gentleman of fallen fortunes; Jean, the philosophic peasant; Janille, the servant; Émile Cardonnet, the young sage; M. de Boisguilbault, the old madman. M. Cardonnet the elder is the only one who is not possessed with the "new idea"; and great care is bestowed in making him the type of the heartless manufacturer (as if this were not a matter of course), whose cold brutality kills his wife, and who crushes ideas as well as men with the grindstone of the factory. All these personages (M. Cardonnet always excepted) have the two inevitable characteristics: heroism of heart and an inexhaustible power of argumentation. Each would perform the finest action and talk the longest. M. Boisguilbault bears the palm.

III.

But at the very time when the humanitarian dream had such cruel possession of her exquisite imagination, she had more than once inwardly and secretly rebelled against the tyranny of systematic friendships and ideas. She had more than once ventured to lift the leaden yoke which crushed her, that she might for an instant breathe the free air of open spaces. Between those two huge Socialistic machines, the *Meunier d'Angibault* and the *Péché de M. Antoine*, she had given to an attentive and enraptured world a delicious idyl, the *Mare au Diable*, introducing by this gem of exquisite purity, this masterpiece in rural poetry, a new manner which was to mark off another period in her career, a period of revival. Unexpected pleasure! In these privileged pages there is no mention of politics or of Utopianism. There is nothing that disunites: only the chaste and tender, only the unaffectedly noble, the simply beautiful, the naturally touching. A little journey of three leagues, which lasts a whole night because the way is lost; a conversation—many times interrupted, resumed, and stopped—between the shrewd ploughman Germain, who is going to seek a wife at Fourche, and the little Marie, who is going to be a shepherdess at *les Ormeaux;* two episodical characters—not therefore unimportant to the action—Petit-Pierre, who would much like Marie for a second mother, and la Grue, the good and handsome mare, for whom one cares as much as if she were a human being; the improvised bivouac under the great oaks, where the night passes so pleasantly—Marie chatters and sleeps, Germain talks and dreams: an emotion which the honest peasant quickly represses in presence of such innocence and candour; and what is better, an excellent project of marriage which dawns on his mind and will be taken to-morrow to the farm;—this is all; it is nothing, yet this *nothing* has found a place in the French literature of the imagination among the perfect works, those brought forth in an *auspicious* hour and consecrated. Poetry is Madame Sand's talisman; as soon as she touches it sympathy revives, and the evil dreams and the weariness fly.

This vein of renewed innocence and poetry was propitious to Madame Sand. After having tried to forget M. de Boisguilbault and his Communism in the brilliant adventures of her *Piccinino*, she lovingly returned to the vein of gold from whence she had already gathered treasures of feeling and grace, and she drew forth *François le Champi*. On opening the book one received a shock. In the very first lines appeared some words of evil augury, some vague theory of knowledge, sensation, and the correspondence which is feeling; and the idea that the lurid light of M. P. Leroux's psychology might be shed abroad in this new work made one tremble. But relief was not long in coming. One breathed again on perceiving that this page was purely digressive, and a final concession to friendship; one breatned again, but the alarm had been great. It was really a *Berrichon* story from beginning to end.

Madame Sand had adapted her fine style to this fancy of the rustic language—imitated to the last degree of nicety, and caught in its very essence—as a vehicle for the history of the worthy Champi and the good Madelon: their bucolic friendship beneath the shadow of the mill —an affection which is that of a mother on Madelon's side, and on Champi's that of a son, but which changes in time by the force of circumstances to a lively tenderness that leads them, arm-in-arm, to the village church, with little Jeannie wearing her slyest smile behind them: is not a child-Ascanius often as necessary in village romances as in epic poems—a pretext for the first effusions of dawning love? But while this tranquil epopee was unfolding itself in the *feuilleton* of the *Journal des Débats*, and even at the moment of the catastrophe of the story, another catastrophe, considerably injuring the first, as Madame Sand tells us, found a place in the *premier Paris* of the said paper. This was the Revolution of 1848.

It was a critical moment for Madame Sand. The emotion of the first hours was nearly fatal to her reviving talent and new turn of thought. That exquisite style was imperilled in the violence of controversy for the sake of certain exacting friends who had attained power; the charming fables with which she had just been enchanting herself and others were for some months replaced by a series of *Lettres au Peuple* and *Bulletins du Ministère de l'Intérieur*. It needed the terrible insurrection of June to break the charm and deliver the captive imagination.

"After those disastrous day," she says, "being agitated and utterly heart-broken by the outward tempest, I strove to recover in solitude, if not calmness, at least faith. . . . In moments such as those, a strong and powerful genius, like Dante, writes with his tears, with his wrath, with his sinews, a terrible poem, a drama full of tortures and lamentations. In our day, the artist who is weaker and more sensitive, who is but the reflection and echo of a generation very like himself, feels the imperious need of turning away his eyes and diverting his imagination by returning to an ideal of calm, of innocence, and of contemplation. In times when the evil springs from the mutual misunderstandings and hatreds of men, the artist's mission is to glorify gentleness, trust, and friendship, thus reminding his hardened or discouraged fellows that pure morals, tender feelings, and primitive equity are, or may still be, of this world. The way of salvation will not be found in direct allusions to existing evils, in an appeal to fermenting passions; a sweet song, the sound of a rustic pipe, a tale to quiet the little children and send them to sleep without fears or suffering,—these are better than the spectacle of actual evils darkened and intensified by fictitious colouring."

These lines were written as an introduction to *La petite Fadette;* they are like a farewell to the turmoil of politics, a low-breathed promise of gentler thoughts in the future. *La petite Fadette* was the first sign of Madame Sand's reconciliation with her genius. In those troublous years, in those uncertain hours, each one of which brought a danger or a menace, fresh discord between the party-leaders or a vibration of the masses, how joyfully did one forget the anxieties of this precarious life in following Madame Sand down the flowery paths (*traînes*) to the river that sleeps beneath the branching trees! How many tears and smiles were called forth (partly because of the contrast of passing events) by the friendship of the two *bessons* of la Bessonnière; the jealousy of Sylvinet; the love, wondering at first, but soon agitated and eager, of the handsome Landry for La Fadette; the growing sweetness of Fanchon, as she is transformed by the magic charm of true love! It was a success due to the reviving grace. The brightest days of her talent had returned, and they were recognised and hailed with general emotion. It is to this rural source of inspiration that some works which are nearer to our time should be attributed; among others, the *Maîtres Sonneurs*, a very original production, and the *Visions de la Nuit dans les Campagnes*, the whimsical fancy of an imagination which delights in interpreting simple terrors, superstitions, and legends, not unthrilled itself by this trickery of fear, which is the poetry of midnight and the nocturnal drama of the fields.

About this time the dramatic passion, which had always been very strong in Madame Sand, awoke in greater intensity; the unfruitful effort of *Cosima* had irritated rather than discouraged it. *Gabrielle, les Sept Cordes de la Lyre, les Mississipiens*, were, in some sort, ideal dramas produced for the pleasure of the imagination. In the studious retreat of Nohant, her favourite recreation with her children and her friends consisted in imaginative dramatic representation, to which each—the *scenario* being previously arranged—brought some improvised effort of his wit, or frolicsome display of her reason, her melancholy, or her gaiety. Her pastoral comedy of *François le Champi* was played in 1849. We will not follow her long in this new direction, one in which the author will never find success worthy of his merit, his effort, his visible desire to do well. The special characteristic of Madame Sand's talent, the love of analysis and poetry, helped her less here than elsewhere. What the drama needs is the science of relief, the instinct of perspective, skill in combination, and above all action, still action, always action; it is the natural gaiety that provokes laughter, the secret of the strong emotions and surprises that thrill the spirit. Lively, rapid action is wanting in Madame Sand; she has neither the dramatic spirit nor the *vis comica*. Her plays lack relief; her art, which is too simple and plain in form, her tendency to delicate analysis and keen reflection, the style itself, which is marvellously easy, but a little prolix and sometimes a little declamatory, at one time only shining by a wise simplicity, at another illuminated by lyric lightning better suited to a novel,—these are so many obstacles to her popularity on the stage. However this may be, during many years, in the last period of her life, from *François le Champi* and *le Mariage de Victorine* (1851) to *le Marquis de Villemer* (1864), Madame Sand was, with unequal success, passionately absorbed in her plays.

She was keenly sensible of the presence in others of the dramatic gift which she valued so highly, and which she made such strenuous efforts to acquire and to have recognised. But whatever may have been said in later times, she was never completely successful. Still, we have witnessed the recent revival of pieces which were at first too hastily abandoned, and they were very favourably received; we have just been applauding * that pretty and romantic comedy, *les Beaux Messieurs de Bois-Doré*, and the sentimental drama *Claudie*, which was a success, notwithstanding Father Remy's antiquated homiletic tone. I am confident that this experiment might be advantageously tried on other pastorals, dramatised as was *François le Champi*, or on the dramas dedicated to the study of artist-souls like *Maître Favilla.* To understand this kind of success, which does honour to the literary public, one should take into account the strong reactionary movement now at work in favour of the idealised drama. Notwithstanding this, and some other reasons resulting from the sentimental charm of the tardily revived author, we are inclined to think that Madame Sand was not twice successful, lastingly successful, as a playwright, in *le Mariage de Victorine* and in *le Marquis de Villemer.* And it is only just to add that in both cases she had a valuable collaborator—in the first piece Sédaine, in the second Alexandre Dumas *fils*.

* May, 1887.

During this period, while the place of the novel was disputed and in some degree usurped by dramatic attempts, Madame Sand did not abandon the line in which lay her true vocation.

IV.

She produced, successively, some novels of the historic kind, such as *les Beaux Messieurs de Bois-Doré*, from which issued, almost immediately, the play of the same name; the strange hallucination, the retrospective dream of antediluvian love and religion, entitled *Évenor et Leucippe;* some agreeable novels, such as *la Filleule*, *Adriani*, *Mont-Revêche*, which appear to us particularly significant in the extremely vivid and careful delineation of character, the graceful variety of the situations, the life of the plot, and above all, in the marked absence of all social theory, the settled determination to return to the pristine conception of the novel as pure from any alien matter of preoccupation.*

Bucolics cannot last for ever. They brought Madame

* Let us cite again, but without pausing, *la Daniella*, a very *romantic* romance; *Narcisse*, *les Dames Vertes*, *l'Homme de Neige*, *Constance Verrier*, *la Famille de Germandre*, *Valvèdre*, *la Ville-Noire*, *Tamaris* (1862); *Mademoiselle de La Quintinie* (1863); *la Confession d'une Jeune Fille* (1865); *Monsieur Sylvestre*, *le Dernier Amour*, *Cadio* (1868); *Mademoiselle Merquem*, *Pierre qui Roule*, *le Château de Pictordu*, *Flamarande*, etc., etc.; then the *Légendes Rustiques*, *Impressions et Souvenirs*, *Autour de la Table*, *Contes d'une Grand'mère*, etc., etc.

Sand a renewed success and a popularity that for a short time rose to the pitch of enthusiasm; there was reason to fear, for an instant, that she would linger over these studies of a peasant life, which had so opportunely freed her from the hateful study of politics. Therefore it was with great pleasure that one saw her returning to the true home of the novel—society as a whole and in its infinite complexity; to-day, though not for long, among the workmen of the Ville-Noire, yesterday in the homely and puritan *salon* of the Obernay family, the day before yesterday in the aristocratic boudoir of the aged Marquise de Villemer, or on the mountains of Auvergne.

In the long series of works that crown the last labours of Madame Sand with a glory which is yet brilliant, though it may sometimes wane, there are two especially deserving the attention of posterity—*Jean de la Roche* and *le Marquis de Villemer*. I have just read these two novels again, and I fell under the influence of their old charm. I felt it almost as intense and as penetrating as in the old days. How many purely imaginative works could stand the second day's trial, when they no longer possess the attraction of the unknown, and that first bloom of novelty which is often so fragile and artificial?

These two works are in George Sand's best manner, and show the progress which the nicest experience of life was able to bring to her first conception of her art while the inspiration was still unchilled by age. The subject of *Jean de là Roche* is perhaps the simplest and most original. It does not escape the species of poetry which condemns every novel to be, more or less, the history of an unhappy love. There will consequently be the same eternal struggle of love with the obstacles that surround it at every step and hinder it from attaining its object. But the novelty here is in the nature of the obstacle. Jean de la Roche is by birth at least Miss Love's equal; his fortune is suitable, and Mr. Butler, thank Heaven, has nothing in common with the barbarous fathers who occupy so much space in novels and dramas with the outbursts of their fury. As all seems favourable to the happiness of this mutual and favoured love, whence comes the obstacle? Whence springs the source of the tears? Miss Love has a child-brother, a terrible child, who, when he finds that his sister is going to be married falls into a kind of despair. He is jealous in his way, chastely, but morbidly jealous. In his silent and stubborn languor, a nervous fever, terrible relapses, lies the knot of the story. The child nearly dies of his jealousy, and as his sister adores him, as she is the impersonation of sacrifice—sacrifice with a smile on her lips—she unhesitatingly immolates her dearest hopes. In the analysis of this child's strange passion lies the originality of the novel. No active struggle can remove an obstacle of this nature; infinite care and attention are needed in the treatment of this sickness of the soul which threatens every moment to snatch away a fragile life; and, most essential of all, a cheerful resignation and the hardest kind of courage—that which does not fear to measure itself with time, and to wait, almost bereft of hope, for a very unlikely change. In the varied incidents through which an ingenious art conducts the interest and sustains it by unceasing gradation and diversity, the way in which all is unravelled at last beneath the delicate hand of the author—the end of the trial of the two valiant souls and its consecration in a happiness which is really the natural result and, as it were, the work of their generous qualities;—in all this is shown the renewed talent of the author. The last part of the novel, the meeting of the disguised and unrecognisable Jean de la Roche with the Butlers; a very picturesque excursion to the Mont-Dore, which gives him the opportunity of ascertaining if he is still loved after five long years of absence and misunderstanding; the tardy repentance of Hope Butler, the expiation offered by him for the harm already done—which, though the child has become a man, is still of a strange and morbid character; the last scenes at once so well-prepared,—all this completes the reader's delight.

We will not give the story of *le Marquis de Villemer;* it is as well known in dramatic as it is in novel form. A drama or a novel with analogous data has often been in difficulties. The history of a governess or a companion is not new either in French or English literature. But what is new here is the analysis of character, which is as clear as it is elegant; still more in the abundance and variety of most charming details of the home-life. What sparkling conversations are those between Caroline de Saint-Geneix and the old *marquise*, a complex person warped by the abuse of social relations, incapable of living alone, incapable even of thought when she is alone, but charming as soon as her mind is in communication with the minds of others,—whose sole joy in life is conversation, which does her the service of putting her ideas in motion, of enlivening them by movement, of drawing her out of herself! The reader cannot fail to be struck with the *grand* air which pervades this charming story from beginning to end, with the attitude and tone of aristocratic life so naturally caught and preserved throughout the novel. This characteristic of Madame Sand's mind has not been sufficiently remarked in her older works. The democratic ideas have blinded and misled us as regards the habit and turn of the style, which is never more natural than in sketches of high life; here it excels without effort and moves with marvellous ease. Let her be compared on this point with Balzac! How easily superior is George Sand!

It is the speciality of really superior minds to be able to continue without repetition and to be capable of self-renewal. All the works of George Sand's last period are not, however, deserving of the same praise. She occasionally betrays traces of fatigue, the most noticeable of which is a prolixity that is not redeemed by a few touches of moral analysis and a few pages of vivid description. It is none the less true that the literary life of Madame Sand, viewed in its full extent, is a marvel of productiveness; she has enchanted with her romances or disturbed with her dreams four or five generations; in numberless public and private catastrophes, she has nearly always been equal to herself; never showing the full capabilities of her art, continually disconcerting criticism, which thinks it has at last grasped her, and always preparing new surprises, while around her and on the road by which she has travelled so much intellectual ruin is heaped, so many fragments, so much unfinished talent struck down by impotence or by ridicule, and in its infatuation unable to see that it has ceased to exist.

During the intervals between the novels, which were the principal work of her life, she found time to concern herself actively, and even in a literary way, with the lives of others; either in relating divers stories to her grand-children—*le Château de Pictordu*, *la Tour de Percemont*, *le Chêne Parlant*, *les Dames Vertes*, *le Diable au Champ*, and the various *Contes d'une Grand'mère*, which show an inexhaustible imagination; or in carelessly inditing, on the edge of the family table, her somewhat vague impressions of the literature of the day; or again, under the influence of intensest emotion, during the terrible year, describing, in a melancholy but virile style, which throbs with patriotism, the public anguish, the private griefs and anxieties. The remainder of this prodigiously active life, if a surplus of a few free minutes could be found in the course of such busy days, was devoted to an indefatigable *Correspondence*, a species of complement kept from day to day of that biography, the *Histoire de ma Vie*, begun on a vast scale, going much too far back in the family genealogy, and stopping much too soon, where the most curious pages abound amid others which are simply exquisite, such as those relating the sojourn at the English convent.

And in this rapid nomenclature how many works are omitted, how many little masterpieces are left in shadow!

We have tried to give the history of Madame Sand's works. It is somewhat like the biography of her talent, divided into four periods: the first (1831-1840), which is that of subjective lyricism, and in which the emotions, repressed in a dreamy and solitary youth, break forth in brilliant and impassioned romances; the second (1840-1848), in which the inspiration is less subjective, the author giving herself to the influence of extrinsic doctrines: this is the period of the systematic novel; the third (1848 to about 1860), which is distinguished by a visible weariness of theories, by a tendency to a simple, artless, true style, by the triumph of the idyl and by the pursuit of a new form of success, a dramatic success; and the last, which embraces the close of this most productive life (1860-1876), and signalises the return to the novel of the first manner, though the ardour is tempered by experience, at times even deadened by age, and a little faded, notwithstanding some masterpieces which endure and seem to protest against this impression by the still youthful vigour and pure inspiration that distinguish them.

CHAPTER III.

THE SOURCES OF GEORGE SAND'S INSPIRATION. THE IDEAS AND FEELINGS.

CAN the principal sources of inspiration of Madame Sand during her long literary life be distinguished with exactness and reduced to a definite number? What were her views on the great subjects of human meditation with which she was so passionately occupied: social laws, love, nature, ideas, the feeling of the divine in the world and in life? How does she control and mingle these diverse inspirations? Did they not occasionally clash and produce some discordant effect, some confusion in her work?

It would certainly be an insupportable piece of pedantry to invoke the light and charming shades of her different novels, to ask of each what it represents in the world, and to reduce to syllogisms these fancies of a mind which is so free and so varied. Madame Sand has no doctrine in the rigorous sense of the word: it is a powerful imagination that overflows at liberty, it is not a theory that develops itself. Besides, with her passion is much stronger and much more vivid than idea; and when a principle, true or false, inspires her, it has always been necessary that it should cease to be an abstraction and become a feeling. It is said that Madame Sand had several masters in philosophy. I am willing to believe it, since she herself allows it to be assumed. But her first master in philosophy was her heart, a master full of illusion and chimeras, and it was only through its medium that the others were able to act and to make themselves heard.

It is therefore not necessary to make a very strict search for Madame Sand's doctrine; we need only analyse her ideas by means of her feelings.

There are three sources of inspiration that seem inexhaustible to Madame Sand—love, the passion of humanity, and the feeling of nature. Several others might be mentioned together with these, but they are gradually absorbed and disappear.

It seems, if we are to believe her, that love is the sole business of life; that life itself—that is to say, action—in nearly all its forms, has no other object or employment. Before one loved one did not live; when one has ceased to love, or to be loved, one has hardly the right to go on living. This alone—loving and being loved—gives a value to existence. I see another motive appearing dimly in the novels of the first manner, very clearly in the novels of the second period—the humanitarian feeling; but this motive yields wholly to the first. In novels such as *le Compagnon du Tour de France*, *la Comtesse de Rudolstadt*, *le Meunier d'Angibault*, it is love who is the supreme instructor in the levelling doctrine.

One may possibly devote oneself to the great work as Count Albert does, but Consuelo is the hoped-for and expected reward of that devotion. The sole aim of manly activity and heroism is to deserve or conquer love. If social opinion or the accidents of life place a gulf between them and the object of their choice, Madame Sand's heroes display inconceivable strength in trying to cross it. And here there is rather a touching idea, which the author has several times worked out with remarkable felicity. What energy is shown by the half-taught peasant Simon in the rude assault of his destiny! To raise himself to Fiamma's level, he would have strength to conquer fortune, talent itself. Mauprat, his heart filled with Edmée's image, will with incredible resolution and pains change from a bandit, a savage, to an honest man and a hero. When there is no gulf to be crossed one folds one's arms and one loves; the inhabitants of the little world governed by Madame Sand's amorous fancy cannot well do anything else. Look at Octave in *Jacques;* it does not even occur to him that life can have other occupations or duties. He has loved Sylvia; when he ceases to love her he loves Fernande. His uselessness in society causes him neither trouble nor remorse; indeed, he does not think about it, or if he does, he disbelieves it. His social function is to love. Heaven knows if he acquits himself of it conscientiously. Bénédict in *Valentine* has no idea, either, that his intelligence or his arm might serve in other ways. His outward life ceases from the day of his meeting with Valentine; he renounces his activity, he gives up his future, he does not consider that existence has its exigencies and duties. He lives with his love and by his love in the immobility of an Oriental ecstasy, which is only disturbed by his raptures or his fits of despair. Love is the reason of life; the right of living ceases when love ceases. They who persist in dragging along the useless burden of an existence without love are feeble souls who have been incapable of a supreme resolution. We may be sure that these inert wills who have not the energy to die have not had the energy of true love. André, after Geneviève's death, walks slowly, feebly on Joseph Marteau's arm, his eyes bent as if he feared to meet his father's glance. "The unhappy man," Madame Sand tells us, "had not had the strength to die." But look at the true heroes of love: they will know how to take leave of life when love takes leave of them. Valentine will die of Bénédict's death. Indiana will not survive her heart. Jacques, betrayed, seeks an unknown death on the glaciers. He for whom love is past has nothing more to do in this world. So the Æsthetes of the world would have it. See the contrast of the ideas of the English philosopher Carlyle on the same subject!—"What he most violently anathematised in Thackeray's novels was that love is there represented (after the French fashion) as extending over the whole of our existence and forming its greatest interest; whereas love, on the contrary (*the thing called love*), is confined to a very small number of the years of man's life, and is even in this insignificant fraction of time but one of the things that occupy man among a multitude of others which are infinitely more important. . . . The truth is that the whole business of love is such a miserable futility, that in a heroic age no one would give himself the trouble of thinking about it, still less of opening his mouth on the subject."* Which is right?

If one should be surprised that love is not only the chief, but almost the only duty in life, Madame Sand will explain it by saying that it comes from God. It is well known that in those days there was a very prevalent fashion of introducing this name into the wildest transports of passion. The French poets treated of the most questionable adventures of the heart in a kind of mysticism. But no poet or novelist has abused the name of God in connexion with love more openly, I will say more candidly, than Madame Sand. There are assuredly noble passions that raise the soul, and as human reason seeks the divine ideal in all that is great and beautiful, one may sometimes, as one feels that a man is exalted, believe in a secret intervention of God in these privileged feelings. But what indiscreet and dangerous enthusiasm is that which would apply this gracious power of Providence to all love, irrespectively of its nature! Of what guilty weaknesses of heart, what treacheries, what moral debasement is it thereby made the accessory! Listen while Madame Sand in her way traces the high origin of love: "What causes the immense superiority of this feeling above all others,

* Mme. Carlyle : *Portraits de Femmes*, by Arvède Barine.

what proves its divine essence, is that it does not proceed from man, that man cannot dispose of it, that he no more gives than he receives it by action of his will; that the human heart receives it from above, doubtless that it may transmit it to the creature chosen from among all others by the design of Heaven; and when an energetic soul has received it, in vain do all human considerations lift up their voice to destroy it; it subsists alone and by its own power. All the auxiliaries that are given to, or rather attracted by it—friendship, trust, sympathy, esteem itself—are but subordinate allies; it created them, it rules over them, it survives them." And a few lines further on she adds: "Had not supreme Providence, which is everywhere in despite of men, presided over this reconciliation? One was necessary to the other: Bénédict to Valentine, that he might impart to her those emotions without which life is incomplete; Valentine to Bénédict, that she might bring rest and consolation to a stormy and troubled life. But society was there between them, and made this choice absurd, guilty, impious! Providence has established the admirable order of nature, man has destroyed it; which is in fault?" That there is a Divine predestination between Bénédict and Valentine I believe with difficulty, but that God intervenes expressly to authorise the very inconstancies of the heart I cannot in conscience allow to Jacques. "I have never tormented my imagination," says he, "to kindle or revive a feeling that does not exist, or one that exists no longer; I have never imposed constancy on myself as a rule. When I have felt that love was dead, I have said so without shame and without remorse, and *have obeyed the Providence that was leading me elsewhere.*" A singular function of Providence this, of calling Jacques to new amours! However, Jacques brings proselytes to his doctrine, and his wife is the first. For later on, when she betrays him, it is religiously done, if I may so speak. Piety had never before been carried so far in adultery. Just imagine the plan which the amiable Femande forms with the view of consecrating his happiness. "Oh! my dear Octave," she writes to her lover, "we shall never spend a single night together, without kneeling down and praying for Jacques." How nicely comforted the husband must have felt!

One ought not to be surprised, according to this, if Madame Sand's heroes believe that in yielding to love they offer a species of worship to God. The lovers in ecstasies suddenly seem as if inspired. When they speak of their joys it is with a kind of religious exultation; they appear to discern therein sacred rites which they perform with a tremulous pride. They are no longer lovers but high-priests.

In how religious a tone does Valreg tell of the improbable happiness that has come to him, of the strange falsehood and cynical heroism with which la Daniella gives herself to him! I will not dwell on this, I merely wish to indicate the dominant note of that singular thanksgiving. The most mystic metaphors crowd beneath his frenzied pen: "A wise virgin calumniating her purity, extinguishing her lamp like a foolish virgin to reassure the guilty and cowardly conscience of him she loves, of him who misunderstands her! But this must be a dream! . . . *I am in a supernatural state. . . . I feel myself as God has made me. Primordial love, the principal effluence of the Divinity, permeates the air that I breathe; it fills my breast. . . . It is like a rare fluid that penetrates and vivifies it. . . . Thus I live by this intellectual sense, which sees, hears, and understands, an order of immutable things which wittingly co-operates in the endless and limitless work of the superior life, the life in God*," etc., etc. Valreg is no longer merely an apostle of love, he is one of the illuminati.

Coming from God love is sacred. To yield to it is an act of piety; to resist it would be sacrilege; to blame it in others, an impiety. Is not the desire of nature the very call of God to His elect of this new species? Is it necessary to add that love justifies itself? It is irresponsible because it is divine. The errors which it brings are treated by the author and her principal characters with the widest indulgence, the most unlimited sympathy. "Marthe," says Eugène (in *Horace*), "what is the reason of this grief? Is it regret for the past, is it fear of the future? You disposed of yourself, you were free; no one has the right to humiliate you." Even those who have some right to complain, as the forsaken husbands, are the first, when they have great souls, to bestow their heroic benediction on the guilty couple. "Do not curse these two lovers," writes Jacques to Sylvia; "they are not guilty if they love each other. Where there is sincere love there is no crime." And elsewhere: "Fernande yields to-day to a passion, deeply rooted in her heart by a year's struggle and resistance; I am forced to admire her, for I could still have loved her if she had yielded to it at the end of a month. No human creature can control love, and no one is guilty in feeling it or in losing it." But where will this indulgence for the errors of love cease? I fear that it extends very far, even as far as the utmost limits to which the free life can extend. I remember unwillingly a very spirited apology (*pro domo suâ*) made by the courtesan Isidora, who proves to Laurent that all the women of pleasure and folly despised by a puerile stoicism are the purest and most powerful types ever produced by nature. Madame Sand might say that Isidora thus speaks from the force of circumstances, or on account of her position, and that we should not discuss too severely the mad thoughts exchanged at a masked ball; be it so; but, further on, in the same book, Laurent descants upon a similar theme, and boldly concludes, before the noble Alice, that corruption is the only outlet left by society to the faculties of a woman, beautiful and intelligent, but born in misery, and the modest Alice answers with painful frankness, "You are right, Laurent." This time the dictum comes from very serious lips.

In all the faults that lead a woman away, even in those which degrade her in the eyes of the world, society is alone guilty—society, which fetters the free movements of God in the soul. This theory may lead one very far. I fear that if it were unhappily taken in earnest the soul would fall into a kind of Oriental fatalism. It is faith in liberty that makes us free. Believe in it vigorously, and you will feel it living and acting within you. Cease to believe in it, and you will sink to the level of the servile souls whom passion drives beneath its iron yoke. We are free to the degree that we believe ourselves to be so, for it is precisely this affirmation of our strength which frees us. This is a dogma of purest philosophy, and it is a religious dogma too; for religion tells us that grace is not refused to him who merits it by effort. I do not pretend that man is impeccable, nor do I wish that opinion should arm itself with a ridiculous severity to chastise his delinquencies; my sole desire is to restore responsibility to its proper place, and prevent the aggravation of weaknesses which are only too real, by protesting against these accommodating doctrines that are eager to absolve them. There is a certain moral greatness even in a fault, if one recognises oneself as the free perpetrator of it, instead of seeking a cowardly excuse in a fatality that one's very belief creates.

Sensual idealism is the secret vice of nearly all love as Madame Sand conceives it. Her heroes rise to the loftiest heights of Platonism. But look deeper into the heart, and you will perceive a refined or violent sensuality which sullies the noblest aspirations. One example will suffice. Lélia is less a woman than a symbol. Pure love must unquestionably be placed among the exalted feelings which she symbolises. Madame Sand wished to give in her the most brilliant expression of idealism in passion. She certainly speaks in most magnificent language when she exclaims: "Love, Sténio, is not what you think; it is not this violent aspiration of all the faculties towards a created being, it is the holy aspiration of the most ethereal part of our soul to the unknown. Limited beings, we ceaselessly try to lull the insatiable desires that consume us; we seek an object around us, and, poor prodigals that we are, adorn our perishable idols with the immaterial beauties revealed to us in our dreams. The emotions of sense are not enough for us. Nature has nothing sufficiently rare in the treasury of her simple joys to quench our thirst for happiness; we want heaven, and it is not ours!" And the speech thus flashed by sublime and impetuous thought, to the infinite continues to soar. The soul, carried along with it, scales the loftiest heights of feeling. But turn the page; the soul descends the mountain. What a scene! How near is Lélia's *great heart* to a fall! Recall the passionate pages that begin thus: "Lélia passed her fingers through Sténio's perfumed locks, and drawing his head to her bosom she covered it with kisses . . . ." There is in these pages such an indefinable mingling of Platonism and voluptuousness—one continually regaining what the other has seized, and the vanquished voluptuousness perpetually returning to mock the Platonism, which is alternately indignant and softened,—there is in this dangerous and too lengthily-described struggle something so irritating to the imagination that I do not hesitate to pronounce Pulchérie, the priestess of pleasure, less immodest in her frenzies than is this sublime Lélia in the hallucinations of her cynical chastity. The noble ideas that appear in the midst of this delirium only heighten the strange wildness. "How fierce and violent does thy heart beat in thy breast, young man! It is well, my child; but does this heart enclose the germ of some manly virtue? Will it go through life without being corrupted or withered? . . . . Thou smilest, my graceful poet; sleep so." I cannot stand this solicitude for Sténio's future virtue in such a moment. Lélia vainly protests against our suspicions; in vain does she declare that she delights in Stenio's beauty with *maternal candour*, with *maternal puerility*. I instinctively mistrust this fictitious candour and maternity.

One of the consequences of the theory on the providential origin of passion is a romantic axiom that love equalises all ranks. Society alone has introduced caste. God has nothing to do with our puerile combinations. Hence we must conclude that in the providential working that predestines one soul to another no consideration is paid to the degrees of the social hierarchy in which chance and prejudice may distribute these souls on their entrance into the world. All are equal before God, therefore all are equal in love, which is His work. So we shall see that Valentine de Raimbault, Marcelle de Blanchemont, Yseult de Villepreux, and very many other noble heroines, seek their ideal beneath the peasant's blouse or the workman's jacket in their great anxiety to raise their humbled brothers and to restore each one to his proper place. This is how marriages of the soul are made in the world of Madame Sand's novels—the two extremities of the social scale must be brought together. It is delightful to her in her imaginative conceptions to draw conditions nearer to each other, and to prepare (as she thinks) the way to the fusion of castes by love.

How much truth is there in this idea? Does love equalise ranks in life as it does in novels? This is one of the delicate questions that do not admit of a positive answer; other judges than men—beings of finer instincts and powers of induction—could alone determine it. If I am to believe certain evidence, this idea of Madame Sand's is very seductive to a woman's imagination. There is, indeed, a tendency to devotedness in love in every woman's heart, somewhat of a chivalrous instinct that exults in the idea of a generous struggle with the undeserved calamities brought about by society or fortune. What feminine soul could, at least in imagination, resist the pleasure of raising a great mind cast into the shade, a gallant heart lost through the chances of an adverse fate in the lower walks of life? But does this heroism exist elsewhere than in dreams? When a woman is nobly born, and is surrounded with the luxury and grandeur which are a natural setting to high social existence, can she, from the region in which she lives, distinguish this disguised gentleman amid the general crowd, and fulfil her destiny by restoring him to his true station? And if by some miraculous chance she should discover him, would circumstances so adapt themselves to her desire that the two hearts between whom the world places a distance more immeasurable than the abysses of the ocean or the immensity of the desert might be united? But supposing these obstacles to be overcome, and the two souls placed in contact with each other by a propitious destiny, will all be finished then? Will not unforeseen and, this time, insurmountable obstacles be suddenly evoked by the mere effect of a more thorough acquaintance? Will love survive the delicate test of familiar intercourse? Consider that one of these souls brings the indelible habits of manner, speech, and tone that are her second nature, and more necessary to her than her primary nature. Consider that the other has a different origin, and that no distinction of heart redeems inexperience or ignorance of social life, which is only sublime in books. Intellectual culture and peculiarly delicate instincts must at least widen the gulf in which the cruelly disappointed love seems nearly swallowed up. It is doubtless true that love does not consult the rules of the social hierarchy, but one can hardly allow that these rules are absolutely inverted. And, to state my thought precisely, I will admit to Madame Sand that Edmée might love Mauprat: he is of her family, and after a few years of attention he will be a thorough gentleman; or that "the last Aldini" might let first her imagination, then her heart, go out to Lelio: he is a celebrated artist, a man of charming mind and noble heart; or again, that Valentine might forgive some roughness of manner in Bénédict: he is a genius in his way, uncultivated only on the surface, and full of natural eloquence and powerful ideas. But I doubt if Madame Sand's great ladies and noble maidens could, elsewhere than in a novel, love, in one instance an ignorant gondolier, in another an illiterate workman; especially as, if they were infatuated in their disproportioned love, they carry their imprudence beyond all bounds, and dream more impossible unions than their love. In all this I merely express doubts and accentuate shades. I suggest questions, but I should be sorry to have to determine them. Who not bereft of reason would dare assert that there is anything which love cannot do? But then some things must be considered as exceptions.

We have indicated Madame Sand's theory of love, if indeed it is not forcing a meaning to see a theory in these fervid aspirations of a boundless sensibility. And after all, and in spite of the justest criticisms, it is difficult to resist the charm. One must keep one's reason strictly on the watch that it may not be carried away. Never were a more eloquent candour and a more enthusiastic fairness brought to the aid of paradox and error. And how unjust it would be to see in Madame Sand only the fascinating painter of the disorders or the sophistries of passion! What great and noble elements there are in her conception of love! What generosity, what delicate pride, what chivalrous devotion in her best loved creations! On some of these rests the undying light of ideal grace. Geneviève, who wert fresher and more pure than the flowers among which thy life glided onwards, until the fatal day that stole thy happiness in troubling thy purity; Consuelo, enchanting and proud, symbol of conscience in art and honour in love, pure maiden so religiously faithful to a memory amid the adventures of your wandering life; Edmée, most winsome type of woman, one of the most touching creations of the modern novel, sweet heroine so often visiting the dreams of young and enthusiastic souls, clad in the fantastic hunting costume in which your wild lover saw you first, with that air of smiling calm, courageous frankness, and inviolable honour; and you also, Marie, heroine of the *Mare au Diable*, you who had but your ingenuousness wherewith to inspire a great love, and with that weapon vanquished the rude soul of a peasant, who by your disinterestedness educated a generosity that was unconscious of its own existence, and whose artless goodness made justice and devotion to blossom where before calculation reigned supreme; finally you, Caroline de Saint-Geneix, who vanquished a more powerful enemy than the roughness of the peasant—the implacable pride of prejudice, and who by means of reserve, purity, and greatness of soul overcame all resistance, softened every heart and transformed all the fatalities of education and race around you: each and all of you loved nobly and delicately, and you have shown us for a day, an hour, true greatness in true love. You have moved the soul of many generations. You will now dwell among that ideal people created of genius, which lives by the immortal breath of art.

Madame Sand's conception of love has not been unimportant: it has produced consequences of a certain significance. It was by the idea of irresponsible passion that her contest with opinion and social laws began, and that this was first introduced into the novels where it afterwards held so considerable a place.

And there is revealed a want in Madame Sand's moral nature which it would be useless not to indicate, as she herself so plainly betrays it. What was needed in her most powerful, most richly enthusiastic soul was a humble moral quality, which she despised and even calumniated when she spoke of it—the quality of resignation, which is not, as she seems to think, the inert virtue of mean souls eager to bow beneath any yoke in their superstitious servility to strength. This is a false and degrading resignation; true resignation proceeds from the conception of the universal order, by reason of which individual sufferings, without ceasing to be a cause of merit, do cease to give the right of revolt. What would become of society if everyone, arming his passion with force, entered the lists with all legitimate interests or contrary rights? It would be the elementary society of Hobbes, the struggle of man become a wolf for man. Resignation understood in its real sense—philosophical and Christian—is a manly acceptance of moral laws and also of the laws necessary to the thorough order of societies; it is a free adherence to order, a sacrifice to which reason consents, the sacrifice of a part of man's individual property or personal liberty, not to force or the tyranny of human caprice, but to the requirements of the general good which subsists only in the accordance of individual liberties and regulated passions. This conception is altogether wanting in Madame Sand. She does not know how to resign herself, and the pride of passion vibrates in all her works, arrogant and unyielding.

Hence those celebrated declamations on the right of the human being to shake off the yoke of social laws, those unpitying and senseless laws that sacrifice the heart and violate liberty. Hence so many angry prophecies and that Utopianism of the ideal marriage. "I do not doubt," exclaims Jacques, "that marriage will be abolished if the human species makes some progress towards justice and reason: a more humane and not less sacred bond will replace it, and will know how to assure the existence of the children born of a man and a woman without ever fettering the liberty of either. But men are too coarse and women too cowardly to ask a nobler law than the iron law which rules them; beings without conscience and without virtue need heavy chains." To ask a law—this is soon explained; a law which shall license the liberty of the husband and wife without destroying the family founded by the compact of those two liberties. Just try to conceive this law in the contradiction of its terms! Unless they simply declare for free union I defy the legislators of the future to escape this dilemma: that either the man and the woman must alienate their liberty, or the family must perish. Still, if there were but the man and the woman to consider, the problem would soon be solved. They would leave each other as soon as their love ceased—always supposing that they could live separate. It is a convenient panacea for the use of each if they both have an income, or even if they have none. But what would become of the children under the law of these ephemeral marriages? Madame Sand does not concern herself with that. Nor does the Sybil when she prepares the decrees of the future in the Temple of the *Invisibles*. "Yes," she says, "the abandonment of two wills which are absorbed in one is a miracle, for every soul is free by virtue of a divine right. Then away with sacrilegious oaths and vulgar laws! Leave them the ideal, and bind them not to reality by the chains of law. *Leave to God the care of continuing the miracle.*" Excellent! but if God should not continue the miracle? If the enthusiasm which impelled this man and this woman to join themselves together by the always revocable compact of love, if the persons which made them exclaim in the first hour of love, "Not in this life only, but in Eternity," —if, in short, passion grows cold and disappears, will the ideal marriage therefore cease? Enthusiasm is a very fragile foundation for the family. The novel *Jacques* shows us a woman who had married in the plenitude of her liberty, who had known and practised the fervour required in ideal marriage, and who too had said, "for Eternity." And yet, a few years later, what becomes of

Fernande and the family that she has founded? Madame Sand eludes the difficulty; she sends the children an illness which carries them off, and she advises Jacques to put an end to himself in some unknown abyss, that his wife may be free to love elsewhere. Well and good; but reality cannot be governed like a novel. And if the children persist in living? And if Jacques declines to die? It would really be too cruel to recommend his example to all husbands whose wives no longer love them. What a hecatomb!

Had George Sand been guilty of such intentions in her first novels? She denied this in a very curious and courteous though strong answer to M. Nisard; it must have been written about 1836, and has been annexed as a postscript to the *Lettres d'un Voyageur.* It is virtually a personal apology for the novels of the first manner and their tendency: "If only the satisfaction of my vanity was concerned," she said to the severe and delicate critic who had been occupied with the social part of her works, "I should have nothing but thanks to offer you; for you bestow on the imaginative part of my stories much more praise than it deserves. But the more I am touched by your approbation the more impossible it is for me to accept your blame on certain points . . . . You say, sir, that hatred of marriage is the purpose of all my books. Allow me to except four or five, among others *Lélia*, which you include in the number of my denunciations of the social institution, though I am not aware that it contains a word on the subject . . . .

Neither did *Indiana*, when I wrote it, appear to me a possible apology for adultery. I think that in this novel (where, if I remember right, there is no adultery committed) the *lover* (*that king of my books*, as you wittily call him) has a worse part than the husband . . . . *André* is neither *against* nor *for* unlawful love . . . . Finally, in *Valentine*, the catastrophe of which is, I admit, neither new nor clever, the old fatality intervenes to prevent the guilty wife from enjoying by a second marriage the happiness for which she could not wait . . . . *Jacques* remains, the only one, I think, happy enough to obtain some attention from you."

And this very clever apology begins by an avowal that the artist may have sinned, that her inexperience and unequal hand may have beguiled her thought, that her history is somewhat like that of Benvenuto Cellini, who attended too much to detail and neglected the form of the proportions of the whole. It is probably something of this kind that happened when she was writing this novel; indeed, all her novels bear traces of the haste of an ardent and unskilful workman who delights in the fancy of the moment, missing the end because he amuses himself with the means. This first excuse once admitted, we should remember that she had more of the poet's than the philosopher's nature: that she does not feel capable of the reformer's work, and that she often wrote *social laws* instead of the words really meant—the *abuses*, *absurdities*, *prejudices*, and *vices* of the time, which seemed to her to belong to the jurisdiction of the novel quite as much as to that of comedy. To those who asked her what she would put in the place of husbands, she naïvely answered *marriage*, in the same way that she thought that priests who had compromised religion should be substituted by religion. She committed, perhaps, another grave fault against language when, in speaking of the *abuses* and *vices* of society, she said *society*; she declares that she never thought of reframing the Constitutional Charter, nor had she had the intention ascribed to her of giving her personal unhappiness to the world by way of proving her thesis, thereby making a social question of a private case. She had confined herself to the development of aphorisms as peremptory as these: "The transgressions of women are often induced by the ferocity and injury of men." "A husband who wantonly despises his duties while swearing, laughing, and drinking is *sometimes* less excusable than the wife who betrays hers in weeping, suffering, and expiating." But what is her conclusion, after all? This love, which she raises on the ruins of the *infamous* and crowns, is evidently her Utopia; this love "is marriage as Jesus made it, as St. Paul explained it, and, if you like, as Chapter VI, Title V of the Civil Code expresses its mutual duties." It is, in a word, the marriage that is at once real, ideal, humanitarian, and Christian, the marriage that is to substitute conjugal fidelity, true rest, and the sacredness of the family for the shameful contract and the stupid despotism engendered by *the decrepitude* of the world.

But the essential objection still remains. How can an irrevocable compact be made from elements as changeable and fleeting as love? How can the social sacrament of marriage have the least chance of stability if it is only secured by passion? Must there not always be the introduction of a more solid and substantial element to act as a basis—either honour or a social oath, or else a religious pledge? And how will the weakness of the abandoned wife or wronged child fare in these dangerously alterable and easily broken unions?

It is possible that Madame Sand finally recognised the force of the objection. Her later novels show a decided improvement. As an instance, look at *Valvèdre*, the counterpart of *Jacques*, which established as a logical conclusion that marriage necessarily falls with love. It is most curious to see the same subject twice treated by a sincere author—the second time after an interval of twenty-seven years—and to observe how the different subjects of thought belonging to the two different periods of life influence the destinies of the heroes of the novels and produce such different catastrophes! The subject is the same: the struggle between the husband and the lover; but how differently it terminates! Unfortunately, *Valvèdre* is not equal to *Jacques*. The spirit and charm are partially eclipsed. Alida is Fernande over again, but Fernande despoiled of her poetry, and coldly, artificially impassioned. The lover is little changed. Whether his name is Octave or Francis, he is the same individual, lavishing heroism in words, and beginning life by sacrificing a woman to his self-love. But the husband is no longer a sublime fool who kills himself that he may not be an obstacle in the life of her whom he loves to madness, that his wife's happiness may not be a crime. Jacques is now called Valvèdre; he has meditated, he has sought consolation in study. He has crushed the madness of despair; he does not give up his right and duty as a husband; he no longer voluntarily gives his wife to Octave; and when she has left him, and is dying of the false situation into which she has been thrown by resentment rather than love, he appears at the dying-bed, and recovers from the feeble and useless lover the heart of the woman who will soon have passed away. He crushes Francis with his generosity, even while he deprives him of the joy of Alida's last thought. The issue is, as we see, exactly opposite to the former novel. Reflection has done its work—and life also.

It is evidently the passionate attack against the laws of marriage which introduced the whole social question, at a later date, into George Sand's novels. She boldly crossed the limits at first assigned to her thought. She was not, as in 1836, checked by the fear of posing as a reformer of society, but undertook to find a remedy for the "infamous decrepitude of the world," at least in the principal points.

Exaggeration in feeling, weakness and incoherence in conception: these are the characteristics of Madame Sand's social theories. We will not dwell on this aspect of her works, which is so well known and has been so often discussed; and there would be many questions of property or of proximity to decide between her and those whom she was pleased to call her masters in the work of destruction and reconstruction that she was elaborating. Besides, we must remember that since this by-gone age of politicians and philosophers whose minds were teeming with future reforms, this part of Madame Sand's novels seems strangely antiquated. When one returns to them after this interval of nearly fifty years, one might be witnessing an exhumation of antediluvian doctrines. Wonderful and magnificent superiority of poetry, which is fiction in art, to Utopianism, which is the exaggerated fiction of social reality! All that is of pure, of disinterested art in the works of this period has preserved through these long years the serenity of an incorruptible and radiant youth. The beloved faces which one sees with so much pleasure in the intervals of the declamatory thesis still people our imagination, and are as the immortal charm of our memory. On the other hand, all that proceeds from the system, all those doctrines which are so deceptive, so vague, so full of specious promises and Sibylline formulæ, all that recalls the grand epopees of the future philosophy, bears the trace of a terrible decay; it is dead, irrevocably dead. Who nowadays would have the courage to read and discuss pages (written, nevertheless, with ardent conviction at the dictation of great prophets) such as those which fill the second volume of *la Comtesse de Rudolstadt*, three-quarters of the *Péché de M. Antoine*, and that *Évenor*, which I cannot bring to mind without indescribable horror? Is it necessary even to recall the fundamental elements of the doctrine, a mixture of an "historical" mysticism elaborated by Pierre Leroux, and a revolutionary radicalism ingeniously imitated from Michel (of Bourges)? Madame Sand always had a strong taste, even a passion for ideas, but she interprets by mingling and confusing them. Her metaphysics are very vague and uncertain. George Sand is certainly an idealist, and it is this that so profouudly distinguishes her from the school of novelists that followed. But who can clearly despise her thought in any of the works in which she tried to express it? She soars on untiring wing towards the regions of mystery, but what precise doctrine does she discover in her sublime explorations? Only try to understand what meaning she would give to the great word God, with which she is so prodigal, in certain solemn circumstances. What becomes of that Name at the end of the transformations which her thought has undergone, in its various phases, under the masters to whom she listened with such docile and passionate curiosity? What does He become in this immense humanitarian laboratory, this God of pure Love to whom Lélia cried in her despairing prayer in the church of the Camaldules, this God of Truth whom Spiridion with glowing love invoked during the persecution of the monks, in the dark visions of the cloister? Under the influence of Pierre Leroux, it seems indeed as if he had become the Beginning and the End of the universal *circulus.* As time goes on, and Madame Sand is delivered from the sect, she will restore to the name of God some of its compromised significance and lost attributes. But it would be no slight matter to relate the Odyssey of this God, successively transformed and annihilated, and finally restored; it might be an Avatar of which the meaning is often very enigmatical.

Far from us be the thought of irony! These are grave matters; to amuse oneself with them would argue a pitiable mirth. Besides, these philosophical and social ideas lived in a sincere spirit, and that alone forbids mockery. I heartily yield my respect, not to the theories themselves, but to the loyal enthusiasm that embraced them. And then, it must be acknowledged that these doctrines are now extinct, and quite extinct; they fell beneath their impotence in the face of facts, and the doctrinal socialism of 1848 has been found unequal to the solution of the simplest problem. But what is not extinct are the problems themselves; what is not extinct is the economic and moral necessity of stating them and seeking at least their partial solution. What is not extinct, in fine, is misery, imprescriptible obligation imposed upon all who have a conscience and a heart to devote a part of their thoughts and of their life to the sufferings of their unknown brothers. That the theories of that time are gone by, I believe; but the cause which produced them survives, and it is not too much to say that it is the cause of Christianity, that these two are but one cause, and that no one is either a Christian or a philosopher who is not resolved to oppose to the sad conquests of misery the growing efforts of sympathy and devotion. Let us not be too anxious to know if the progress is unlimited and continuous. We do know that it is not spontaneous, and that it depends on us. To work for a partial progress, on an atom of space, in a second of time, is perhaps all that we can do: let us do it; being less careful to love the humanity of the future than that which is near us, within reach of our hand and our heart. There is nothing new in this: it is the socialism of charity, and it is the best.

Which is the nearer, we or Madame Sand, to M. de Lamennais, the only real philosopher she ever knew? Had she read these admirable lines in the *Œuvres Posthumes?*—"There is no more dangerous way of deceiving men than by representing happiness to be the end of the earthly life. Happiness is not of this world, and to imagine that we shall find it here is the surest way of losing the enjoyment of the good things which God has put within cur reach. We have a great and holy function to discharge, one that obliges us to a stern and perpetual combat. We nourish the people with envy and hatred, that is to say, with sufferings, by contrasting the supposed felicity of the wealthy with their anguish and misery." And with an admirable soul-gesture the illustrious thinker exclaims: "I have been near them, I have seen these rich people who are so happy! Their savourless pleasures end in an irremediable disgust that has given me an idea of the infernal tortures. There are, doubtless, rich people who more or less escape this fate, but the means of escape are not procurable by wealth. Peace of mind is the foundation of true happiness, and this peace is the fruit of duty perfectly fulfilled, of moderation in desire, of holy hopes, of pure affections. Nothing high, nothing beautiful, nothing good can be done on earth but at the cost of suffering and self-denial, and sacrifice only is fruitful!" For this simple page of a real thinker, who tempers his wrath and indignation with such forcible reasoning, I would willingly give all the speeches of Pierre Leroux, and above all the famous conversation that took place one evening, when the Tuileries were sparkling with the brightness of a fête on the Pont des Saints-Pères, when M. Michel (of Bourges) endeavoured to initiate with fierce doctrines the truly simple mind of Madame Sand, when she was amazed and almost scandalised by the furious eloquence lashed in that moment with a species of Apocalyptic ferocity. Can anyone deny that genius has its simplicity, since, despite the horror which she confessed to feeling at this conversation in frantic dithyrambs, Madame Sand still continued to believe in the political sagacity of her prolix and noisy friend?

For my part I shall never forgive this friend and many others for having stirred to factitious excitement an artist-sensibility so alive to strong impression, or for having thrown that vivid imagination into the chimerical violence of their doctrines. After all, they had a ready accomplice in her heart, and it was long in perceiving how easy is the transmutation of reforming ideas into preposterous Utopianism. She afterwards acknowledged this herself. Her heart was the first dupe.

As a little child in the fields of Berry, and later at the convent, most decided in the first indications of her nature were an immense kindness, an infinite compassion, a deep tenderness for all human sorrow. Even with the strongest prejudices it was impossible to approach her without being disarmed by the beaming grace of the feeling. She was rarely angry either with things or people, even though they might cause her grievous pain: she would withdraw sadly, but without anger, from the connexions or situations that were most hurtful to her dignity. And when she glanced around her it was with a look of deep and tender sympathy. After having tried many systems of morality, which she thought might be suited to her needs, she finally formed one for herself, consisting in this one rule: Be good. Everyone forms his own system of morals as he thinks best. From the day when she rose to this clear conception of the end and use of life, the profound emotions which had agitated hers to its depths were calmed; a higher light had penetrated the trouble and tumult of her heart, which until then had been guided only by easily deceived instincts. This idea (which really summarises the social morality) had with her assumed great importance and a kind of intellectual royalty—*the duty of coming out of oneself.* She had learnt by painful experience the inexorable selfishness of passion. She had learnt that the true life is the thinking, not perpetually of oneself and for oneself, but of others and for others; and further, of all that is great, noble, and beautiful, all that can divert one from that *self* which is always ready to be the object of its monotonous analysis and its dismal idolatry.

It is by this noble side of her nature, the ever-ready sensibility and the absolute goodness, that she had been so easily carried away by the social theses emerging from the brain of every unattached reformer. What were they, indeed, but varied forms of the Utopia which had attracted her from childhood onwards, and in which the principal motive-power had been the deep feeling of human ills, of social ills: a Utopia which was innocent and holy as long as it did not seek to reign outside the imagination and the heart, or try force as a last means of Apostleship?

"There is nothing strong in me," she said one day, "but the need of loving." It is by this need of loving that she succeeded in preserving, above all temptations of doubt and even slightly against the opinion of her century, "which did not just then tend in that direction," a wholly ideal and emotional doctrine which was rather like a Christian Platonism. Leibnitz first, Lamennais, Lessing, then Herder interpreted by Quinet, Pierre Leroux, and lastly, Jean Raynaud—these are the teachers who by their successive help kept her from too much fluctuation in her various trials of modern philosophy. "Any help from the wisdom of the masters is opportune in this world, where no conclusion is absolute and definitive. When, with the youth of my time, I was shaking the leaden vault of mysteries, Lamennais happily came to sustain the sacred portions of the Temple. When, indignant after the September laws, we were ready again to overthrow the reserved sanctuary, Leroux came, eloquent, *ingenious*, *sublime*, to promise us the reign of Heaven on the very earth we were cursing. And in these days, while we were still despairing, Raynaud, already great, rose greater than ever, to open to us in the name of Science and Faith, in the names of Leibnitz and Jesus, the infinity of worlds as a native country which reclaims us." What different and contradictory names successively invoked!

She had not received so much of this help as to destroy her faith in some of the ideas which, clothed in more or less varying forms, give value to life and meaning to hope. After the period of devotion and ecstasy through which she had passed at the English convent, and the following years of wavering, which ended at last in a rupture with the ancient faith, she had suffered great perplexity and great dejection. She had known doubt, and the state of her soul was revealed in several of her books.

"You ask me," she says to one of the real or imaginary friends who are the convenient confidantes of the *Voyageur*, "if this book (*Lélia*) which you have read so seriously, is a comedy:—I answer *yes* and *no*, according to the days. There were nights of contemplation, austere grief, and enthusiastic resignation when I wrote fine passages in good faith. There were mornings of weariness, sleeplessness, and anger, when I scoffed at my mood of the previous night, and thought out all the blasphemies that I wrote. There were afternoons of ironical and facetious humour, when I took pleasure in making Trenmor (the convict philosopher) more hollow than a gourd." All her creations had, at a certain moment, represented the different moods of her mind in its conflict. The characters are neither wholly real nor wholly allegorical. Pulchérie is Epicureanism, inheriting the worldly and frivolous part of the last century; Sténio, the enthusiasm and the weakness of a time without distinctive mark or support; Magnus, the remains of a corrupted and brutalised clergy; Lélia, the sublime inspiration that is the very essence of lofty minds. Such was her plan; how far she succeeded in its execution, in what degree she brought it forth from the semi-reality in which all the characters move, sometimes to entrust it with an offensive reality, must be decided by the artist—it is the artist's work, the artist's responsibility. As to the philosophic idea which dominates the book, it is evident in every page; the idea was conceived "under the influence of profound despondency," called forth by the enigma of life, which had never weighed upon her more heavily and more grievously. She was surprised at the storm which greeted this book, not understanding that the author is hated through his work. It was a book written in good faith, that is, in sincere doubt: such a doubt as stirs souls and ideas to unfathomable depths. Those who did not understand or hear this cry of conscience, this broken wail mingled with sobs and delirium, were scandalised.

During the whole of her life she was infallibly and always consoled in the hour of distress by the love of nature—one of the rare loves which never deceive us. This love was her surest inspiration, and the half at least of her genius. No one, with words, simple words chosen and intermingled, such words as we all use, and which express common feelings with hopeless coldness—no one has succeeded as she has done in interpreting in the living reality of a landscape the lights and shades, the harmonies and contrasts, the magic of sound, the symphonies of colour, the depths and the distances of woods, the infinite movement of the sea, the infinite star-spangled sky. And above all, no one has succeeded as she has succeeded in seizing and expressing that inward soul, the secret soul of things which sheds the charm of life on the mysterious face of nature.

What causes this superiority as a painter of nature that strikes us at once in Madame Sand? The first reason that suggests itself is so simple that I hardly dare to express it. Madame Sand sees nature, she looks, she does not invent. We can prove this by the clearness of details and of the whole, which makes us see exactly what she sees herself. The reader's thought easily reconstructs the grand scenes sketched by her broad and flexible brush. I found the explanation of this effect, which is so rare though it is so simple, in these lines jotted down at the bottom of a lost page: "It is certain," says Madame Sand, "that what one sees is not always equal to what one dreams. But this is only true in the matter of human work and art. For my part, whether it be that my imagination is usually idle, or that God has more talent than I (which is not impossible), I have generally found nature infinitely more beautiful than I had imagined; and I never remember finding her moody except in hours when I was moody myself." It is a special characteristic in Madame Sand that she has an imagination which does not precede her look, does not deflower her pleasure, and does not interpose between her and nature the play of a subjective prism. Madame Sand sees nature as she is; she looks long and deeply. She indelibly engraves the picture that has been before her eyes; it is preserved unaltered. One might say that it is less imagination than the imaginative memory which she brings to bear upon her remembrances and visions of reality. It is just this absence of a brilliant defect that gives such luminous precision to the features of her landscapes. M. de Lamartine, one of the great word-painters of her time, had too much splendour in his soul to see clearly without; I venture to say that he always found nature less beautiful than he had anticipated. The brightness of the dream eclipsed the reality, and then, when he wished to recall and paint the landscape of which he had had a glimpse, his imagination still worked as much as his memory. His picturing was magnificent but confused; it had the scintillating mobility f a radiation, so that the dazzled gaze could not fasten on it or distinguish anything tranquilly.

Art after a time wearies the mind. Nature always refreshes it. When Madame Sand was travelling in Italy, her travelling-companion, Alfred de Musset, was eager about nothing but "hewn marble." "Who," people said of him, "is this young man who is so anxious about the whiteness of marble?" At the end of a few days he was satiated with statues, frescoes, churches, and galleries. The remembrance of some clear cold water in which he had bathed his weary, heated brow in a garden at Genoa was sweeter to him than any other. "It is because the creations of art speak to the mind alone, whereas the spectacle of nature speaks to all the faculties. It enters at every pore, as it does through every idea. To the wholly intellectual feeling of admiration the aspect of the country adds sensual pleasure. The coolness of waters, the fragrance of plants, the harmonies of the wind, circulate in the blood and nerves at the same time that the brightness of colours and the beauty of forms creep into the imagination."

The whole of nature passes into man, speaking to him in the most varied language. There are some pages at the end ot the first volume of *la Daniella* which are a wonderfu attempt to express the orchestral effect, which intelligent ears can realise, of the combined and sonorous murmurs of the country. At nightfall Jean Valreg goes up to the little terrace of the Château of Mondragon, and there he collects all the sounds that ascend to him from hill and valley; he studies the music produced by the meeting of the scattered sounds, constituting in that part of the country a natural, local music. "There are," he says, "places that always sing," and he finds this the most melodious of all. Then in very curious language he enumerates the different noises—the song of the great vanes, which is so regularly phrased at the beginning that he has been able to write six perfectly musical measures which invariably return at each breath of the east wind. These whimpering, doting vanes, with their notes of an impossible tenuity, are like the high tenors that dominate the whole. "I know not what spirit of the air attunes them to the sound of the Camaldules bells . . . . other songs are mingled with these noises—the choruses of peasants dispersed in the fields. . . . The continued bass is in the deep whispers of the unrhythmic pines and the cascade which gathers to itself the lost waters of the ruins. Then there are the cries of birds—vultures, and especially eagles." In listening to all this Valreg pursues an idea that has often struck him in connexion with the natural harmony produced by chance: by the very reason that they escape defined rules, they produce effects of extraordinary meaning and power; they fill the air with a fantastic symphony which is as the mysterious language of the Infinite.

The discovered or divined reality of scenery is joined in Madame Sand with a charm of wholly individual sensibility and attraction. One is not merely interested in her delineation, one is touched by it, one loves it. This new effect results from the delicate art, or rather, happy instinct, that never describes for the sake of describing, and always associates with nature something of the human soul—a thought, or a feeling. The landscape is never solitary with her: it is chosen in harmony or in contrast with the soul breathed into it. But the contrast itself is a kind of special and more subtle harmony. Just when it seems that in the imposing solitude of the mountain all else is forgotten, a little Spanish shepherd girl will spring up from the shadow of a rock, and we put into a corner of the landscape her delicious profile, her pretty smile, her floating hair, "mingling with the breeze like the tail of a young mare." And the soul, on seeing the human face, once more unbends from that too austere grandeur induced by the peaks and torrents. If our gaze is lost in the remoteness of them, a sail is pointed out to us, and beneath that sail we imagine a rough worker who toils and suffers. If it is raised to the illimitable depths of the sky, we are led to fancy numbers of unknown beings animating the blue immensity with their joys and sorrows. There is ever a touch of feeling in the landscape; it adds to the infiniteness of nature the more mysterious infiniteness of the soul. Such charming touches as this continually appear in the dialogues or reflections: "In putting my hands to my face I perceived the scent of a sage-plant of which I had touched the leaves a few hours before. I had respected it; I had only taken from it this exquisite scent. Why did the plant leave it? What a precious thing is perfume, which, without causing the plant it emanates from to lose anything, attaches itself to the hands of a friend, following him on his journey to charm him and long recall the beauty of the flower he loves! The perfume of the soul is remembrance." This page has always struck me as an example of the happy facility with which Madame Sand associates a soul with things and man with nature.

One never forgets these scenes. They match so well with the situation of the novel or with the spirit of its characters that the two memories are inseparably joined, and ere long make but one. Is it possible to think of Valentine without going back to that enchanting scene where her soul, vaguely impatient of love, presses its mysterious call in the deserted country, which she is crossing alone on the evening of the fête, at her horse's negligent pace, when suddenly to the murmurs of the adjacent waters and rising breeze is joined a pure voice, a young and thrilling song! It is Bénédict approaching, it is the meeting, it is love; destiny has done its work. And André—which of us would not know where to find him if he were missing?

He is sure to be there, in that uninhabited gorge where the river flows silently between two verdant banks, indulging the dreams of his romantic and troubled adolescence. He is there, I saw him, evoking his heroines Alice and Diana Vernon, behind that group of aspens into which, one day, he thought a shadow, a fairy passed: it will be Geneviève. There are attitudes that are engraved on the mind. "He wrapped me in my coverlet of pink satin and carried me to the window. A cry of joy and admiration broke from me at the sight of the sublime scene spread out before my eyes. This wild and romantic sight delights me to distraction . . . . Ah! let us alter nothing in the places that you love, Jacques. How should I have other tastes than yours? Can you think that I have eyes of my own?" Thus wrote, thus spoke Fernande; and later on, when Octave has come into her life and Jacques is betrayed, we shall involuntarily see her again at that window from which she saw her rich domain, and we shall seize in that attitude and moment the ready ecstasies of a weak soul. . . . Mauprat! his very name evokes the sinister shade of his ruined castle, the portcullis destroyed, the traces of fire still fresh on the walls, the vault where Edmée's courage failed nearly filled up. Lastly, Sténio, the charming poet—go and see him for the last time in the first sleep that was not troubled by the proud and stormy vision of Lélia. There he is, laved by the blue wave, his feet buried in the sand of the shore, his head resting on a carpet of lotus, his eyes fixed on the sky.

Thus all these memories return to us in the happy setting that first received and has ever fixed them. All George Sand's novels are epitomised in a situation and in a landscape the poetic nicety of which nothing can break or disturb. Man associated with nature, nature associated with man—this is a great artistic law. No limner has practised it with surer and more delicate instinct.

For nature really crushes us with her silence and her grandeur when the voice of man is not there to touch her, when her mute harmonies do not express an imaginary soul which ours conceives and interprets. Man, Madame Sand has somewhere said, is not made to live always with trees and stones, or even with the waters which flow through the flowers or the mountains; he must live with man, his fellow. In the stormy days of youth one dreams of living in the desert; one fancies that solitude is the great refuge in injury, the great remedy for the wounds that will be received in the battle of life. It is a grave error. Experience will soon undeceive us, teaching that where we do not live with our kind no poetical admiration or artistic enjoyment can fill up the gulf. It is thought, it is suffering, it is the human gift of feeling or loving which breathe life into nature and create the landscape with the particular soul that contemplates it. But nature helps this work of idealisation by lending her forms, her harmonies, her colours: and all these combined become the immortal material of art.

In passion and nature Madame Sand is supreme. All beyond this twofold inspiration is strange to her, as if, so to speak, it proceeded from an exterior soul; and if the forms of her talent lend themselves in their admirable pliancy to some new inspiration that does not come from the very heart, one soon feels the effect and the pre-determination. She is justly herself, in the plenitude of her powers and the liberty of her art, only when she tells of the delicate agitation of dawning love, of the violent emotions of hearts tried by life; or in her bold sketches of Alpine scenery, as in the journey to the Pyrenees,* or of the life and aspect of Venice, as in the *Lettres d'un Voyageur*, the peaceful scenes of the Berry country, of which the vision pursues her through all the enchantments of Italy. She reaches the climax of her art when she unites the two inspirations, and, by infusing the human soul into nature, gives a tender touch to the landscape and adds sympathy to grandeur.

This love of nature is not only to be attributed to the school of Jean-Jacques Rousseau, it proceeded from herself. She had felt the holy greatness of the earth, the fruitful foster-mother; her Virgilian spirit had lived, during great part of her childhood and youth, in fellowship with the fields and woods; she was truly the daughter of that native soil which had cradled her in its furrows, fed her with the little *pastours*, fashioned her in its image, formed her by its familiar influences, consoled her in many causeless troubles, charmed her with its vague terrors. By this communion of feeling she had made herself the sister of the little peasants with whom through long months she had lived in roving companionship, and who since then had grown up. Hence came, most naturally, her taste

* *Histoire de ma Vie*, vol. viii.

for the bucolic and the idyl which appears in nearly all her works, even becoming, at one moment of her life, a refuge in the violent emotion of politics, and, as it were, a privileged vein. Then, confronted by the social injustices that had wounded her, she will evoke the spirit of rural life and the picture of rustic homes; from the stage of the world which she has judged to be artificial, she will transfer to as human and more natural a stage (in her thinking) the conflict of passions and the dramas of the heart that she is ever pursuing. But she will also transfer some of the illusions of her imagination; she will often see only embellished or rectified types—the poet-peasant, priest of nature, officiating and blessing the labours of the field, or the virtuous peasant-girl, sentimental, chivalrous, even heroic (like Jeanne, the *grande pastoure*). This is certainly poetry; it is so sincere that it seems natural. Balzac and the modern novelists will have a different idea of the peasants, and will sketch them with a hard and even savage roughness of touch: is not this exaggeration in another way? What I would more willingly censure in George Sand is, not her delineation of the superior peasant—who after all is a reality, provided that one helps him a little to emerge from a casing of vulgar impressions and feelings—but her chimerical conception of the philosophic and learned peasant, like Patience, who is rather a fugitive from society, a renegade of towns, a Jean-Jacques Rousseau taking refuge in the forests; he has nothing of the elementary soul of the fields.

But George Sand's slightly-idealised peasant is not as untrue as has been said: this combination of excellent feelings and germs of poetry may be found in him in certain circumstances and by some happy discovery. The author has merely detached them from their native roughness and interpreted them by language. She has not created, but expressed them. All her rustic characters are, in a strict sense, possible; to become what they are in her romances they only need a favourable opportunity, an outward excitement, a combination of events which may raise them above their ordinary way of feeling and speaking, and thus bringing a self-revelation. This is the work of the artist, who, to speak correctly, does not invent, but adds to the human reality the consciousness by which it perceives itself, and the voice by which it accounts for and explains itself to others. This is the peculiar work of George Sand in her adorable sketches of peasant-life. She is rather an interpreter than a creator, if one excepts some false and artificial characters which have nothing of the peasant but the appearance and the name, and are introduced into her sheep-fold by a species of fraud.

CHAPTER IV.

GEORGE SAND'S INVENTION AND OBSERVATION.—HER STYLE.—WHAT MUST PERISH AND WHAT WILL SURVIVE IN HER LIFE-WORK.

WHAT part does Madame Sand give to imagination, what part to observation? How does her most rich and most varied inventive power combine with her experience of life in the different situations described, in the characters put in action? The question has often been thus cursorily decided: an idealist and a romanticist, Madame Sand does not observe.

This is easily said; but it would be a mistake to suppose that these faculties are always irreconcilable and divided—concluding therefrom that there are two schools of novelists radically opposed to each other, that of George Sand and that of Balzac. It would hardly be paradoxical to declare that Madame Sand observes very closely, and that Balzac, on the other hand, imagines with a kind of intrepidity. In fact, it is very possible that there are not two conflicting schools in literature, as people are fond of asserting—that of imagination, or idealism; that of observation, or realism. For my part, I attach but indifferent importance to these arbitrary distinctions of programme, and these various and absolute claims. In fact, it is even possible that there are no schools in literature, in the strict sense of the term; merely different temperaments, organised more especially for observation or imagination: one more alive to exactness of detail, the other giving free play to the inventive power. A school is artificially created when a man of either temperament, having in some sort made trial of his powers of origination or success, constitutes himself, some fine day, the master of a style. He is so accepted by numbers of inferior minds, who adopt the watchword and follow his lead, exaggerating the *manner* of the initiator, and being docile to success, which often reveals the changing taste of opinion. So is a system made—merely with the idiosyncrasies, and especially the defects of a man.

These school disputations seem to us vain. There was originally no absolute difference of opinion between Madame Sand and Balzac, whom she had met several times during her novitiate in Paris. She says herself, with a very easy eclecticism and witty tolerance, that every manner is good and every subject fruitful to him who knows how to use them. "It is fortunate," she said, "that it should be so. If there were but one doctrine in art, art would soon perish for want of boldness and of new ventures."

Balzac was a living proof in support of her theory. "She pursued the idealisation of the feeling which formed the subject of her novel, whereas Balzac sacrificed that ideal to the truth of his delineation." But he was careful not to make of this sacrifice the programme of a school; it was simply a tendency of his mind which he thus expressed. More liberal than his disciples were afterwards, he recognised the right of the contrary tendency, and congratulated Madame Sand on her faithfulness to it. Thus did these two great artists preserve justice and tolerance towards each other. Besides, Balzac, on his side, was by no means the slave of a dogma. He tried his hand at everything; he himself searched and felt his way. It was not until much later that the school, having formed itself, ascribed to the leader as an absolute system what had at first been merely a preference of taste.

This may be said with even greater truth of the dynasties which have followed Balzac; the principal chiefs of these dynasties have confined themselves to recasting in programmes their predominant mental qualities:—for example, Flaubert, a man of a single masterpiece of immense elaboration; or the brothers Goncourt, two artists in acute and subtle sensation; Alphonse Daudet, whose profound and cruel observation has such hold on the minds of his time; or again, Zola, who has created the epopee of the ultra-democratic novel, the master of the *Assommoir* and *Germinal;* to the recent advent of Paul Bourget and Guy de Maupassant: one a keen psychologist suffering from the "evil of life," the other endowed with a natural humour and a thoroughbred style which but ill-conceal a fearful depth of contempt for man and, perhaps, if one penetrates further, an almost tragical sadness. In reality, can it be said that each of these names represents a school? Assuredly not; we should see, instead, an infinite diversity of minds, each of which attributes to itself the origination and arrogates the sovereignty of a new style; there are variations of style in individual minds, as, at certain moments, there are variations of taste in the general mind. Fashions last but for a time; they succeed, without destroying and even without replacing each other, in a species of regular rhythm. No one can tell in what direction the next generation will tend, when all are tired of the excesses of a brutal observation. Perhaps there may be a return to George Sand, who is for the moment too much neglected by an exclusively positive epoch enamoured of facts more than ideas, delighting in experimental methods, even where they have no place, and distrustful of beautiful chimeras. Even now there are symptoms, apparent to watchful minds, of a reaction towards the creator of so many delightful novels.

George Sand was drawn by the particular cast of her mind to the conception of adventures, more or less chimerical, and the conflict of ideal passions with imaginary events: herein lay her keenest pleasure. But it would be the greatest mistake to suppose that she was a superficial observer of real life, and that it rarely inspired her. What strong proof we could give of the contrary! Can it be said that she was not at once a marvellous artist of superb inventive power, and a profound psychologist in nearly all her works, or at least in certain portions of them? Even at the dawn of her literary life, when her first novels were being written, what fine and varied observation she shows! what a deeply felt experience of life is revealed! And although this is less manifest, less displayed on the surface than with Balzac, yet it is most delicate and of justest tone until the chimera takes possession of the author, and bears her away with the reader to the heaven above or the depths below.

Do you remember, to take one of the first novels at random, the icy family-group in the little *castel* of La Brie? How well it is seen, how subtly observed! How carefully all the various attitudes have been noted in an exact memory! How finely all the details of the home are rendered! How one feels that the rainy autumn evening, following a still more monotonous day, is lying heavy on all the actors! That antique drawing-room, furnished in the style of Louis XV, which Colonel Delmare paces in the spasmodic gravity of his ill-humour; that young Creole, so thin, so pale—Indiana—half-hidden by the mantel-piece, her elbow on her knee, in her first attitude of sadness, not yet in revolt, though ready to be so at the first signal of passion; opposite to her Ralph, motionless, petrified, as if he feared to break the stillness of the scene, just as, throughout the novel, he will fear to disturb events by his modest personality, until events impose on him an heroic part which will find him ready,—is there not in each of these touches an evidence of personal experience, an impress of real life, a preparation of the destinies about to be accomplished? How curious also (in another work, near to this in date) is the psychology of André; that naïve sensibility, inwardly passionate, outwardly fearful, that tenderness of heart which made him half-penitent even under undeserved reproaches! This is an admirable study of character. The insurmountable languor of this personage, his weak and melancholy inertness, his fear of recrimination, his vague and feverish eagerness for the unknown,—does not all this make him the inevitable victim of the conflict that will destroy his life, the conflict between the father, the Marquis de Morand, a good-humoured tyrant, a cheerful, honest blockhead, and his mistress, Geneviève, a poor florist, who will take all that disinherited heart and will die of that love! There is not a page here, not a line that does not strictly belong to the experimental novel—save the poetry that transfigures the whole, even the analysis and the observation. We might pursue the same inquiry, obtaining the same result even, to *Jean de la Roche* and the *Marquis de Villemer;* insisting on this point: that the situations given and the characters portrayed are nearly always taken from the most closely observed reality; and that it is only later, under the pressure of an imagination which no longer restrains itself, that the characters deteriorate and are distorted or idealised to excess.

One of her novels especially, one of which she says herself that it is "an entirely analytical and meditative book," seems to me to stand out in relief upon the ground of her life-work as one of the most powerful studies that have ever been made of one of the morbid forms of love—jealousy: I mean *Lucrezia Floriani.* It matters little that it is a chapter of private psychology, where the real actors in the drama of her life may be recognised under new names. It matters still less that George Sand feebly denied having intended to draw very exact portraits in this novel.* What does matter is the truth of the moral painting which she has given us, whoever the actual model may have been. The starting-point is one of those passions held to be impossible, and which in reality burst forth in the greatest intensity. "How could Prince Karoll—a man so handsome, so young, so chaste, so pious, so poetical, so fervent, and so refined in all his thoughts, in all his affections, in his whole conduct—have fallen beneath the sway of a woman worn with so many passions, disabused of so many things, sceptical and rebellious as regarded all that he most respected, and credulous to fanaticism as regarded all that he had ever denied and ever would deny?" It was in truth a terrible mistake; the punishment was not far off. Scarcely is the destiny of this improbable love accomplished, when Prince Karoll's ima-

* "It has been asserted that in this novel I drew the character of Chopin with great exactness under the name of Prince Karoll. This mistake was made because people thought that they recognised some of his characteristics, and, proceeding by this method, which is too easy to be reliable, they went astray in all sincerity." (*Histoire de ma Vie*, vol. x, p. 231.)

gination begins to work upon all the circumstances of Lucrezia's life, even upon that past which has not been concealed from him ; difficulties begin ; all is darkened in the soul where suspicion has entered ; the life of these two beings is henceforth one long storm.

How jealousy is born, how it infuses its secret poison into the fleeting joys of this happiness, which is at first astonished at itself—how it corrupts this happiness without destroying it, producing brief transports, frenzied agonies, wrath which bursts forth or kills with its long silences—how the moral ruins accumulate beneath the strokes of a madman, and then the fatal, vulgar, and poignant catastrophe,—all this is told with a deductive logic, a certainty of touch, and a depth of analysis which betray that life has been closely observed and profoundly felt. Prince Karoll's malady is an incurable jealousy of the past. The details and gradation of the disease are noted with an accuracy that is almost scientific. He has loved this woman, knowing all and notwithstanding all ; he has loved her when she was no longer either very young or very beautiful, and despite a character which is directly opposed to his own ; never is he able to resign himself to those imprudent manners, those extravagant fits of devotion, that weakness of heart joined to that boldness of mind which seem a violent protestation against all the principles and feelings that have hitherto made his life. He will pursue her with his growing madness, which finally becomes almost furious, even to the day when she falls, without having for a single hour inspired her strange lover with confidence, without having conquered his esteem, without having ceased to be loved as a mistress, never as a friend. Let those who deny George Sand's faculty of analysis turn again to this novel and say whether it is not a profound and admirable study of passion, whether each page is not written with an observation or a memory?

What has led to the belief in the absence of the observing faculty in George Sand is, that there is a point in her finest works when an excessive proportion of the romantic is introduced, entirely absorbing the novel and eclipsing all beside. Romanticism is an excessive enthusiasm in the chimerical: it fixes the age of a generation or the date of a book. It may be recognised in the manner of loving (especially in the way of declaring one's love), in the manner of conceiving and imagining events, and in the more or less agitated and over-excited manner of writing.

A master in criticism, M. Brunetière, has laid strong emphasis on these characteristics. "Her whole romantic generation loved in this furious fashion. All the world does not love in the same way—each has his own way of loving; but the romanticists loved as no one has loved before or since. . . . Certainly, *Indiana*, *Valentine*, even *Lélia*, and *Jacques* are curious studies of romantic love. George Sand, according to her instinct, took but one starting point or fulcrum from reality, and abandoned it immediately, that she might return to the interior dream of her imagination. . . . There is in these novels a romantic and sentimental element that has become strangely out of date."*

Let us take—from the beginning in each case—two of the most celebrated works, *Valentine* and *Mauprat*, and see how this judgment is verified, and also how the prognostication is fulfilled. Each of these books contains novel, rich, and varied matter, naturally imagined, and as like the real as is possible—soon mingled with exaggerations of character and detail which startle or disgust the most docile and credulous imagination. That the enchanting Edmée should love her cousin Bernard; that she should love him from the moment of her meeting him in the terrible society of the Mauprats; that she should have tacitly chosen this boor, this barbarian who can scarcely sign his name; that she should have set herself the task of civilising him that he might become worthy of her; that she should finally succeed by her active and silent devotion in making him an estimable man and a gentleman, by raising him to the level of his own heart: all this is the very essence of the novel—and what a fine, what a noble novel!

But with the diverging or meeting currents of these two existences, originally separated by an unfathomable gulf, but drawn together in life by the most sincere love, glides the improbable element, ever increasing, interrupting the interest, disturbing the pure and beautiful emotions of the novel, and hindering their free develop-

* *Revue des Deux Mondes:* Literary Review, January 1st, 1887.

ment. This is the perpetual apparition of the old man Patience at all the cross-roads of the neighbourhood and in every page of the novel; it is the inevitable interference of this man, who has learnt everything in the life of the fields, and knows all that can be known about the present and the future,—this great justiciary, this impromptu magistrate, who silences all the provincial powers,—this peasant who on every possible occasion plays the part of Mirabeau, guiding events by his eloquence, arranging and disarranging the action;—is he not the personification of artificiality and improbability? Who will deliver us from this factitious character, with its loquacity and infallibility? It is really asking too much of our goodwill to expect it to accept this prolix collaborator, illuminated by the glare of the coming revolution, working in the name of the social contract towards the justification of Bernard, who is not guilty, and towards the climax of the novel, which would be reached extremely well without his help. This is the romantic element; it is the more blamable here that it is quite useless. The worthy Patience seems to me decidedly to play the part of the Fly or the Coach-wheel; and the active speechlessness of Marcasse does ten times as much work without appearing to do so, although he too has a good deal of the romantic about him.

Valentine is, with *Mauprat*, one of the most charming and most tragical of love-stories. For what should we ask of Madame Sand? In reality, love is the only thing she understands. Here again abound the most wondrous sketches of love, enshrined in the scene of her long and continual dreams, the Berry country, which she so dearly loved. The incomparable grace of her brush betrays the *incognito* of the modest scenery of the *Vallée-Noire*, of which she says: "It was myself, it was the frame, the vesture of my own existence." And all this she gives to the public as if attracted by a secret charm which she must shed abroad in her turn. Hence proceeds that analysis of passion which is not to be forgotten, which makes every reader Bénédict's accomplice. One follows him, one sees him stop, his gaze fixed on Valentine, standing on the bank of the Indre; and sitting on an ash-tree, he abandons himself to the fascination of that figure, now reflected in the still water, now broken by the rippling wave. He does not think in that moment, he enjoys, he is happy; his eyes drink in the deadly poison that will kill him. The events develop in due course; but now, little by little, some of the already indicated characters change and become distorted. Bénédict is the sublime and impassioned peasant. M. de Lansac, Valentine's betrothed, though originally an honourable gentleman, becomes first the slightly exaggerated and gradually the excessively degraded type of the man of the world—without a generous feeling, without moral youth, worn and withered within, covetous and dissolute; in short, he becomes all that is needed to make the struggle hard to Valentine and easy to Bénédict. Madame de Raimbault, at first simply a prejudiced woman of the world, suddenly appears as an elderly coquette, a frequenter of the balls at the *sous-préfecture;* divesting herself to an improbable extent of her interest in her daughter, as does also M. de Lansac, later on, of his interest in his wife—doubtless that the gravest events may be tranquilly developed unhindered by the family-life, when the simplest restraint would fetter the free movement of the novel. This must explain the perpetual coming and going of the most compromising and most easily compromised personages who enter the park and the château, or leave them as they please, all day long and even at night. Bénédict avails himself of this liberty to his heart's content, first in order to attempt the treacherous murder, on the very evening of the marriage, of the husband, M. de Lansac, under the astonishing pretext of punishing "an unfeeling mother who coldly condemned her daughter to a *legal shame*, to the deepest shame a woman can know," afterwards, to introduce himself furtively into the château to take the vacant place of M. de Lansac. Thereupon ensues—one of the most astonishing and wildest fancies that ever crossed an excited imagination—the supreme scene of the bridal-night between Valentine, ill, distraught, thrown by her despair into a kind of somnambulism, and Bénédict, who spends near her the troubled hours of the night, intoxicated by the beloved presence, abandoning himself to all the transports of passion, which are happily transformed by a series of accidents into an inoffensive and frenzied soliloquy. All this is very strange. "It must not be forgotten," says Madame Sand ingenuously, "that Bénédict's was an extravagant and exceptional nature."

He will prove this to the end, in numberless incidents, surprises, and frustrated meetings, even in the absurd murder, the blow from a pitchfork that puts an end to the hero by a ridiculous mistake. All this second part of the novel is a series of vulgar and preposterous dramas, in which the improbable destroys the interest. The charm has fled. But how great, how irresistible it was in the first part of the book!

George Sand was herself conscious of this strange impulsion which urged her to exaggerated romanticism: "I confess," she says, in the preface to *Lucrezia Floriani*, "that I delight in romantic adventures, surprises, intrigue, *action*, in a word. . . . But I have nevertheless done my utmost to keep the literature of my time on a passable road between the peaceful lake and the torrent . . . . My instinct would have led me to the abysses,—I feel this still in the interest and unthinking avidity with which my eyes and ears seek the drama; but when I return to my calmed thought I do as the reader does: I recur to what I have seen and heard, and ask the *how* and the *why* of the action which has moved me and carried me away. I then perceive crude improbabilities or insufficient reasons for the facts that the torrent of the imagination has swept away before it in defiance of the obstacles of sense or moral truth. Hence the retrograde movement which drives me back to the calm and monotonous lake of analysis."

We might adopt this method of examination in the greater number of George Sand's novels, fixing the varying proportion of the two elements that she employs, —chimera carried to excess and reality keenly observed. It is here that the great defect of her glorious creative-power would be revealed. She does not understand the composition of a work; she does not know either how to preserve the unity of the subject, which often changes, or unity of tone in the characters, which continually alter. She decides neither the aim nor the proportions beforehand. When she does happen to preserve the unity of the work, it is done unconsciously and as if by special grace. She conceived her characters in a given situation, which was nearly always a state of passion; she became enamoured of them, she interested herself ardently and personally in them; and while they were being shadowed forth and embodied in the inward flame, she would abandon herself to a kind of chance inspiration, which produced the great struggles, controlling it so little, as she tells us, that she did not know beforehand how these battles of life would end, or how the novel would culminate. It was a real triumph of what has since been called the *unconscious* element in talent or genius. Indeed, I cannot better express this singular phenomenon revealed in her method of work than by saying that it was a phenomenon of superb unconsciousness, but very uncertain in its results. Apparently nothing was calculated, nothing premeditated—even the broad lines were not fixed; things happened in her art as they do in life. When a dramatic encounter takes place, when a great adventure begins, who can tell, in life, what may happen on the morrow? So it was in the domain of her imagination. She did not know the day before what would become of or happen to her heroes. She delivered them up to the fatality of her art as life delivers them up to the fatality of events. Hence the striking contrasts in her works—the spirit, the passion, the marvellous preludes, the enchanting opening of nearly all her finest romances. Then comes a moment when a *weariness* is felt: the richness in development becomes prolixity, the story lags in useless digressions and the style grows weary and careless. Still there must be a conclusion—so the story is brought to an end; but it is a conclusion of reason, not of inspiration. The composition languishes simply because there has been no preconcerted plan, and this being so, that it is not sustained to the end by the ardour of thought or passion. The climax never equals the prelude. One saw her intensely preoccupied with the idea of a novel, possessed with her subject to such a degree that all those she had treated previously seemed no longer to exist for her; and then, a short time afterwards, she would hasten to take leave of her dearest creations of yesterday. She had worn away and, as it were, consumed her most beautiful dream-children in the fire of her imagination; she thrust them back into the past, I might say into nothingness, immediately. For was it not a relative nothingness this forgetfulness that with her so quickly followed in the real presence of those beings whose very names would sometimes fade from her memory? The ardent furnace had died down; to rekindle the fire she looked for other types, other models from whence a new world would spring into life.

When the chimerical element thus obtrudes itself in her works and forces events and characters, it is a proof that the inspiration is exhausted, that fatigue begins to be felt, and that the author experiences a desire to have done with the subject of which she has already expressed the substance and the flower. But care must be taken not to confuse this mediocre romanticism which is a sign of weariness in her talent, with another species of romanticism which, with her, produces exquisite conceptions, and is an enchanting device of the imagination. To accentuate this distinction two names will suffice (we could mention ten): *Teverino* and *le Secrétaire Intime.* They both spring from an hour of happy fecundity, and seem to have been finished under the influence of the same fresh and unweary inspiration—from the first page to the last there is no interval for repose or fatigue. Dreams of a summer-night, airy visions of a spring day—one hardly knows what to call these magic creations of the brain that take one to a slightly-ideal world where everything happens according to the author's desire, and where circumstances co-operate and characters adapt themselves in a way that is not usual in this world. *Le Secrétaire Intime* is a fancy "which came to her after having re-read the *Contes Fantastiques* of Hoffmann; it retains somewhat of its origin. All is improbable in this principality erected between heaven and earth by the orders of the enigmatical and enchanting sovereign, Quintilia Cavalcanti, alternately intoxicated with luxury and pleasure, and given up to the most serious labour of thought, suspected of the darkest crimes of love, a Marguerite de Bourgogne who is shown in an enchanted frame—then, suddenly revealed in the midst of the most irreconcilable adventures as an admirable and virtuous wife, faithful to the husband she adores in the *incognito* of her wandering exile. Honourable love with a reckless air! Madame Sand's dream at last realised! It is the only way, it seems, in which marriage can be made bearable. And what a series of trials for the young Comte de Saint-Julien, who finds himself by an accident of travel enwrapped in a mystery, admitted on the highroad into the Princess's coach, to the great displeasure of her reader and the Abbé, and to the stupefaction of the little imaginary and agitated court to which he comes as an event—rising in rank and in favour with a rapidity that intoxicates him, and in that fatal intoxication conceiving an impossible love which leads him to the verge of the greatest perils. The climax arrives. The happy husband, the mysterious Marx, saves Julien from his imprudence. Our hero quits the scene of enchantment by turns enraptured, terrified, humiliated, and wounded. The cure will not be completed until later, after the indispensable illness which follows great prostration of soul, and the return home, where he will bring a calmer imagination, a more indulgent spirit, and the memory, or rather the dream of the adventures which for a year have been to him dazzling and tragical reality. There is no sense in this fable. But what a delicious continuation of Hoffmann's *Contes!* This is how a great artist imitates and is inspired.

Teverino proceeds from the same happily romantic source. So it seems that George Sand, weary of mean and commonplace existence, often determined to escape from it at any cost, telling herself wonderful stories like those that formed so large a part of her life as a child, and made for her a dream-life which was almost as important and ten times more precious to her than the other. It was on one of these days when she was amusing and delighting herself with her stories, like Scheherazade in the *Thousand and One Nights*—though it was to satisfy the caprice of her own imagination, not that of a ferocious Sultan—that she conceived the idea of this unique day; and, once conceived as if in a dream, it was thrown on paper in the perfection of its life and freshness, which were scarcely dashed by the almost insensible work of composition.

There is certainly cause to exclaim at the improbable when one sees, among other incidents, the organisation of that picturesque caravan at Sabina's villa at sunrise. Léonce intreats Sabina to let him take her wherever he likes—without telling her anything beforehand—through the most wild scenery, as far as they can go in the day. He has touched the magic chord, the unknown; fancy overcomes the last resistance, and Léonce is to be the disposer of that day. They start together with Sabina's negress and the jockey on the box. Then begin the various encounters; they take up a good *curé* who is gravely walking along with his breviary in his hand; a little further on wanders a sweet little peasant-girl, whose speciality is the taming of birds: her they also annex to the caravan; and at last, after a thousand adventures, the hero of the romance appears—the most singular and marvellous of heroes—a traveller whom Léonce finds bathing in a lake, and whose appearance in his noble nudity is very different from that which he presented a moment before in his sordid rags. Léonce makes a gentleman of him by throwing him some suitable clothing. A touching apologue, which shows us that the difference between men is very often merely a difference of habiliments, especially in Madame Sand's novels. It is one of the author's favourite ideas, and she will often return to it, though so happily and gracefully. Teverino reveals himself to Léonce in all his natural distinction; he is the handsomest of mortals and the most eloquent of artists. Thenceforward he will take his place, the first place, in this romantic journey; he shows superiority in every way—as virtuoso, philosopher, devoted friend (although an improvised one), and chivalrous lover,—occupies all the rest of the day, all the evening which ends it and the morning which renews it, with the most subtle, brilliant, and poetical talk, the most audacious actions and the boldest ventures of the heart,—always, however, checked in time with a discretion that a man of the world would not show. He dazzles with his artist-voice all the little Italian town in which they pass the evening; he astonishes Léonce more and more, even irritating, though at the same time dominating him by his noble conduct; for a moment he almost charms the elegant and haughty Sabina into loving him, and it is only in his generosity that, after troubling it as if to prove his power, he loosens from himself the fragile heart which has been for an instant surprised, returns it to Léonce, and disappears. This improvised sovereign of a few hours in this singular journey of a day is a spoilt child of George Sand. He is indeed the artist-adventurer in whom she has always delighted, one of those Bohemian-geniuses—ragged but refined, haughty and noble—who owe their rich talents to nature and have preserved them carefully, thanks to an independence, an idleness, and a disinterestedness which make them poor but keep them pure. She has seen him act with her own eyes, this time; she has seen him advance, she has seen him commanding the little world into which she introduced him. She has been happy as at the success of a beloved son of her imagination. One may smile at her simple happiness; but the touches of real life are so well combined with the fable, there are such charming incidents in this day arranged by a most benevolent and ingenious providence, there are such elegant and refined conversations, that we must perforce submit to the author's fancy. And it would be really very ungracious to resist the charm which penetrates and fascinates us.

The novel thus conceived is simply poetry. I grant it. But is there anything untoward in this, and will George Sand lose by such an accusation? The novel must either be allied to poetry or to science. The scientific novel is in high favour at the present day: the science of manners, of institutions, of social classes, of characters and temperaments, of the physiological and medical influences that determine the individuality of each of us, of the heredity that affects successive generations—here is the indefinite and ever-varying matter of the experimental novel. But must we sacrifice to this species of novel all others, particularly that which is treated at once as a work of analysis and poetry—as George Sand instinctively judged that the novel should be? Let us take heed: the novel according to George Sand is the national novel of France; if we are to believe the interpreters of the sources of French literature,* it proceeds from the old *chansons de geste;* it belongs to the family of poetry. Besides, who can prove that this conception of it is wrong?

* "A *romance* in the middle ages was simply a composition in the Romance language—in French, that is; and especially—as the compositions held most in honour are the *chansons de geste*—does it bear the same meaning as the *chanson dė geste.* At the end of the middle ages it means successively a *chanson de geste* in prose (a romance of chivalry), a prose-history of some great adventures invented at will, and finally, a story invented at will. Try to find, in the last evolution of the meaning, the poetry in a novel!" (A. Darmesteter, *la Vie des Mots*, p. 16.)

The improbabilities that abound in George Sand's works of fiction are noted with pedantic exactness. But would it not be easy, in opposition to the improbability of events which may be indicated in her writings, to note the want of logic in the characters, the incoherence of feeling, the morbid singularity of conduct under pretext of disease or heredity, in the writings of the most admired naturalistic authors? We should soon ask ourselves where the greater improbability was. It will be a dispute of long duration, and we have no intention of entering therein. But it would be interesting to know whether the supposed observers of reality do not make quite as many concessions as the other novelist to a certain conventionality as artificial, as arbitrary, and as false as that of which they complain so bitterly in the school which they wish to destroy—as if tastes and dispositions could be destroyed!

In this way of understanding the novel the style is concerned, and it deserves a special study as regards George Sand; but we shall merely indicate a few of its characteristics, easily recognisable in the infinite variety of subjects of which she treated in the long course of her life, which for forty-six years was absorbed in the most fruitful work.

It certainly cannot be said that she was not receiving her education as a writer during as long an interval of time, or that she did not modify her medium of expression and her resources. Nevertheless, her language was formed at the first attempt, it was already ample, flexible, full of movement and fire. The long practice of a literary life merely developed, but did not create it: it came to her instinctively when, in her retreat of Nohant, she first jotted down, on a few scattered pages, her sorrows, her tears, her rebellions, the whole matter of her secret dreams. Words already obeyed her without resistance, similes followed spontaneously and combined with each other without effort, and with an accuracy which only the finest writers achieve at the first trial. To write, is for some natures as natural as to breathe. George Sand wrote in prose as Lamartine did in verse: it seemed to them both a function of life, they discharged without having studied it, and would both have been unable to account for it either to themselves or to others. Neither of them was an artist by work or by will; each was an artist by nature—born a greater writer, and such from the first page.

This facility, which is a gift, is also a snare. George Sand does not escape the peril of too heedlessly abandoning herself to the current of thought which carries her away. She has an excessive pleasure in developing her ideas; she occasionally loses and forgets herself in a kind of prolixity that deceived her; she has certain carelessnesses. Also, a tendency to bombast has been so often remarked that there must be some ground for the accusation. In the conversations, or rather the speeches arranged in dialogue—*Lélia* or *Spiridion*, *Consuelo* or *la Comtesse de Rudolstadt*—this beautiful style unquestionably becomes the prey of a gloomy philosophical lyricism, is dissolved into fleeting vapours, or grows dark in a half-wilful obscurity. Darkness does not suit the healthy and natural tone of the writer. She gladly shakes it off when the philosophical crisis is passed, and is herself again—either in descriptions of scenery, which in *Lélia* are wonderfully artistic, or in the delineation of character. Directly she has passed from the semi-real and unsubstantial regions, directly she touches land, directly she betakes herself to life, or amuses herself in a situation which she has invented (such as the different meetings with the wayfarers in *Teverino*), there the dialogue is most animated and sparkling, and also most graceful, and some of the remarks and conversations are full of a polished and elegant wit, even when the society is equivocal. The quality of wit in George Sand's style has not, perhaps, been sufficiently remarked. "The romanticists," it has been said, "did not understand fun: neither Châteaubriand, nor Lamartine, nor Vigny, nor Hugo, nor Balzac, nor George Sand." This is not quite correct as regards Madame Sand. She was not witty in conversation: she did know how to season her talk with humour. But as soon as she took pen in hand all was different. She rapidly followed the conversations which she mentally heard, and the improvisations of her imaginary interlocutors abounded in simplicity, grace, spirit, and ingenious delicacy; the force of the situation was so vividly present with her that she seemed but to echo it. But the inward soul that dictated this brilliant and fine repartee was her own: it was *herself*, and *another* very different from the self of real life.

"It is not," we have again been told, "by an extraordinary brilliancy or by a plastic perfection that her style recommends itself to us, but rather by qualities which proceed from goodness and are related to it. For it is broad, easy, generous, and no expression seems to characterise it better than this of the ancients: "*Lactea ubertas*—an abundance of milk, a copious and beneficent flow from a generous udder"; and the similitude calls forth a daring and charming invocation to the "*sweet Io of the contemporary novel.*" Certainly nothing could be more pleasing. It is a mark of homage from one of the younger writers who have the most deeply and sincerely appreciated her. But one word disquiets us. This style, which is so full of expression and colour, is considered not to be sufficiently *plastic*. What is meant by this? Doubtless that it is not distinctively moulded on actual forms; that their outlines are not rigorously enough defined (as in Victor Hugo, Théophile Gautier, or Flaubert); that it does not study to bring them into relief? Is this a mistake? If it is not plastic—sculptured, that is—it is nevertheless very picturesque, and when employed in description it is like a beautiful painting. Is not this a compensation? It is of a marvellous transparency through which one sees the reality as the artist saw it, *plus* the thought of the artist who interpreted it. Whether in description or in analysis, or in the course of events, it follows the idea with an unbroken movement, and expresses and manifests it with an ease and fluidity that do not preclude strength.*

I have seen in the recesses of the Jura mountains a spring which is called the Blue Spring on account of its colour; it reflects the surrounding landscape, the patch of sky above it, and possibly also the nature of the rock in which it has hollowed its azure cup. It is calm, deep; it attracts as if by a magic charm. One cannot see this spring without being fascinated by it and adoring the naïad who consecrates it; one follows it as it escapes into the adjoining meadows; it excites itself by the declivity which it obeys; it bubbles noisily in its rapid descent on its pebbly bed; it chafes and murmurs, at the bottom of the slope, at a brutal and immovable rock that obstructs its way; it diverts its anger and its course from this barrier, murmuring still, and at every turn extending its waters, swollen by the neighbouring torrents, which it receives and absorbs. For an instant, as if brimming over with the accumulated treasures of the strange waters, it overflows its banks, it exhausts itself by the overflow, it also loses part of its superfluous waves among some islets of gravel; then, finally collecting itself by a last effort, it gathers its waters together, and offers itself in renewed calm to the contemplation of men, after having borne on its crystal wave so many mobile landscapes and varied scenes of town and field. It is an image of George Sand's style, which is always faithful to the

* M. Jules Lemaître, *Revue Bleue*, January 8th, 1887.

interior movement of her thought, interpreting and depicting it in its flights and agitations as well as in its sudden tranquillisation.

They have considerable reason on their side who tell us that in the lapse of these forty or fifty years the style, in a certain measure at least, has become antiquated, like other portions of her work. There is, in fact, a complete apparatus of extrinsic ideas, factitious sentiments, and language proper to every generation, giving one the same impression, when one sees it again in the light of day, as a faded dress or disused garment. This law of inevitable decadence—which merely affects the outward part of the human being, the passing choice that he has made in his day of certain ways of being or seeming—has not spared in Madame Sand any of the sentimental element, the romantic in the extravagant expression of feeling or invention of situations, the exaggerated improbability of events, the passion of theses, the superabundant declamation, the excesses of a too lyrical style at which the author would herself occasionally smile. This is the effete and condemned part of the work: it has foundered, and in any other writer would have inevitably made shipwreck of the whole.

But here, the loss of so many works, portions of which at least are superior, and sketches on which the ray of art has rested, would have been a disaster indeed. How much will remain and revive, though an unjust forgetfulness may have temporarily misapprehended it! All that is of easy grace, elegant creation, enchanted reverie, sincere passion, marvellous fancy—all this surely deserves to live. Time will certainly do its work, here as elsewhere.

And after the process of elimination, to which with unerring precision it subjects every great reputation, it will confer immortal honour on the power of invention that does not exclude the faculty of analysis, but makes a wondrous setting for it, and will proclaim that, owing to the inexhaustible wealth of imagination and expressive gift of style, George Sand will live as a poet who has few equals, one of the greatest poets of her race and of her time.

We are now able, it would seem, to answer the question propounded in the first line of this study. Yes, there will be a return to Madame Sand after a few years of neglect and a few necessary eliminations in her work. She will attract new generations by the brilliancy of the poetry which we have tried to define. If she merely consoled us by some of her works, in the excess and inundation of the contemporary naturalism, she would have had ground for writing even for us, even for what is called posterity. She will take her place in the sure revival of the novel, the drama, and the poetry of idealism, which will long find favour with the humanity of the immediate and remote future whatever be the check to the spiritual impulse.

The habits of the present day give a very important place in life to the novel. But nothing obliges us to believe that this place will be eternally occupied by the naturalistic novel. As we have already said, there will be a division between the two opposed theories, or possibly a periodical oscillation of the general mind between them. The literary kingship of the novel is in great part owing to the modern *weariness*—a malady which was less severe in other centuries less excited and more believing than our own; it is tedium, the absolute void in mind and heart, which is the universal characteristic of modern man. Formerly people amused or occupied themselves in the intervals of the daily toil either with the passion of wit and conversation, as in the eighteenth century; with religions passions, as in the seventeenth century; or with the violent curiosity excited by the Reformation and the Renaissance, as in the sixteenth century. Now when life is overstrained in the toil of business, and compelled to repose, what resources remain to it in the vast desert of ideas which represents the moral and intellectual world to the majority of mankind? The novel now holds the place occupied in remoter centuries by controversial questions, in the last century by questions of criticism and social renovation. The exaggerated development of positive life has at the same time produced an irresistible desire to escape from it. Nothing—no, nothing, not even the desire of speedily making a fortune and applying that rapidly gained fortune to rapidly succeeding pleasures—can repress certain needs of the mind. In vain does one offer to modern man the refreshment of violent pastimes or amusements; one succeeds, indeed, in pleasing him for the moment, in stimulating him for an hour or two, but as his activity is drawn to outward objects he becomes excited and exhausted. Just when one thinks him most forgetful of the inner self, he escapes from the exterior influences, makes sudden retreats, and returns to that self, weary of the life o yesterday, of the life that will be to-morrow. And then, being long unused to thought, he soon becomes fearful of the inanimate solitude, the silence that he finds within him; he has forgotten to fill and adorn with solid thoughts those deeper depths of the soul in which he rarely dwells. The philosophical or religious ideal seldom revisits that soul which is devoted to easy and vulgar divinities. Severe studies alarm the mind that has remained barren under its layer of superficial culture. What is there that will for a moment fill the terrible void before him? The drama, and also the novel, which only differs from the drama in the development of the action concentrated on the interior stage. Besides, the novel is always there, always ready to his hand; it is fitted to fill certain hours when man, alone with himself, can only think. He takes such and such a work which has made some noise in the world, he leaves it, he returns to it as fancy dictates. The novel seems to adapt itself spontaneously to these unoccupied intervals of modern life: it fills the hours of rest from action or business, in which even the most ordinary man feels an inexpressible, vague weariness, or some gloomy disquietude that seems like a need of thought.

But the influence of the novel does not end here; it is not merely the companion and the intellectual recreation of empty or indifferently cultivated minds. The profoundest intellects do not escape from it: it is a kind of habit created by the mind. I once asked a distinguished philosopher of the times what article he generally read first in the *Revue des Deux Mondes*. He answered ingenuously that he always began with the novel. M. Guizot, who had the gravest mind of his time, whom one always imagined as being naturally absorbed in the loftiest philosophic or religious meditation, told me that he worked during the earlier part of the day, that he then went out for his walk as the weather allowed, and that at four o'clock on every day of his life he came in to have an English novel read to him. But it is chiefly in the life of young people and women that the novel has introduced or imposed itself as the principal food of the mind. It may indeed be said that for many it is the only literature.

And this seems the natural place for the wish, or the hope, if one likes it better, that George Sand may be revived as one of the unjustly forgotten masters. If one thinks that the novel might be something more than a humble diversion for a mind in distress, the element of vulgar curiosity, if it must, like other forms of art, purchase its sovereignty by a lofty end, justify it—in a word, have an aim—would not the condition be that it should bring the ideal into this poor life which is so agitated in appearance, so over-excited outwardly, so noisy on the surface, so dreary and joyless within? And would it not be opposing this aim to proscribe that ideal of factitious life which is played before our imagination, as it is, and very carefully, proscribed in real life? And what art is that, if it is art at all, which gives us a succession of degraded types, situations alternately gloomy and violent, trivial scenes, and common or odious scandals, under colour of studies of manners, of the representation of the realities which beset our every-day life, which occupy and pursue our attention? The incurable vice of the novel thus understood would seem to be the negation of its legitimate aim, which is to raise mankind for a moment above the sadness and misery, the trivialities and tedium of every-day life, and to take him for a few hours into a world where he may at least change the course of his ideas and his commonplace cares, where feelings have more strength, characters more unity, passions more nobility, love more loftiness and duration, the sun more brightness. The English novel, which has long been acclimatised in France, and the Russian novel, which has recently made so proud and triumphant an entry into French literature, are much nearer this conception than might be imagined. The two most recent forms of the novel, whether in George Eliot or Tolstoï, join to a foundation of realism, which is demanded by the natural needs of the modern mind, severe aspirations and lofty aims that bring them singularly near, in certain points, to the ideal just described.

We have seen that this was also George Sand's idea of the novel at the dawn of her literary career.* To

* See Chapter II.

transform the reality of characters and passions by raising it above vulgarity and deformity, above all, to fear to degrade it in the sport of events—what is this but to seek by every possible means the most complete and enchanting expression of the dream of life, to bring the light of the ideal into our sad and colourless existence? Is not this art—an art which is great and true? Our life on earth is hard, says George Sand, and we shall never be so satisfied with ourselves and with others as not to wish to lose ourselves in day-dreams. No one has more freely and more fully taught us the enchantments of this dream. We shall never quench the thirst for fiction unless our world is transformed into a paradise where the ideal of a better life will no longer be possible. In the meantime we shall always desire to escape from ourselves: our imagination will always find a charm, a delicious intoxication in this delightful draught, poetry in the varied forms of an art, the poem, the drama, or the novel. What will become of me if, instead of this exquisite draught, your unpitying hand pours me out a second time the common draught which has disgusted me? It is George Sand's glory that in the course of her long career she always escaped this peril, and always spared her unknown friends this fearful after-taste. On this point at least she never deceived them.

CHAPTER V.

HOME-LIFE AT NOHANT.

GEORGE SAND'S METHOD OF WORK.—HER LAST CONCEPTION OF ART.

BEFORE taking leave of George Sand, let us glance back at her private life, and study her for a moment from that stand-point. Without such a study it is not possible to form an exact idea of an author, more especially if that author be a woman. This life cannot be said to begin before George Sand's final installation at Nohant in 1839, after the journey in Switzerland with Liszt and Madame d'Agoult, and a few months' retreat in Majorca with the great composer Chopin (who was even then very ill). She did, indeed, pay several long visits to Paris, at intervals, for the education of her children, Maurice and Solange; still, from that date (1839) Nohant really became her home, her centre of action. It was there that she realised her dream of a settled life for herself, her children, and her friends, and it was there also, amid settled and familiar surroundings, that what may be called her *last manner*—upon which we desire to fix the reader's attention—was developed and perfected.

We must, however, recall some of the chief points in the previous life—that which has been the object or the pretext of so many legends. In connexion with this, one should bring to mind Alfred de Musset's charming sketch, *l'Histoire d'un Merle blanc.* All that happened in Paris and in Venice about 1833-1834 was a very old story, but it gives precision to the outset and the drift of that life which was at first so fantastic and adventurous. One finds everything—even the history of others—in this slightly veiled but transparent fancy of the poet in relating the misunderstandings which greet his entrance into life: the ill-will which his own family bears him on account of his unwonted plumage and unusual note, the innumerable accidents and deceptions which make him feel, each day that he lives, how very painful (although glorious) it is to be in this world "an exceptional blackbird."

After numerous adventures, in which he each time loses many of his illusions and a few of his feathers, he at last finds consolation in the shape of the lady of his dreams, the ideal lady-blackbird. "Accept my hand without delay; let us be married without ceremony in the English fashion, and start for Switzerland." "That is not at all my idea," answered my young love; "I wish that my bridal should be magnificent, and that all the fairly well-born blackbirds in France should be solemnly called together for the occasion." Notwithstanding this, the marriage is celebrated in the English fashion—though there is a great assemblage of feathered artists—and they leave for Switzerland, Venice, and other places. "I was then wholly unaware that my beloved had any claims to authorship. She confessed this after a short time, and even went so far as to show me the manuscript of a novel in which she had imitated Walter Scott and Scarron. My pleasure at this charming surprise can be better imagined than described. . . . From that moment we worked together. While I composed my verses she scribbled over reams of paper. I recited my verses to her, and this did not in the least interfere with her writing. She never altered a line, nor did she form any plan before setting to work. She was the type of the literary blackbird." Many features in this sketch are true of the original, but one is quite out of keeping with the physiognomy of the woman-novelist. At no time was her pen —so free in the region of ideas—sullied by caricature or parody. We can believe that the literary blackbird reminded her lover of Scott and his broad and powerful works; but we are aghast when the unjust satirist joins to that name the name of Scarron. Even in her most daring thoughts Lélia is Lélia still, and no quibble or cynical jest ever weighed down that buoyant wing which delighted in soaring and in light.

We will not finish the story, of which the other side may be seen in *Elle et Lui*. She is sad in both these sketches—she was so in reality, and the world knows it well enough. With such matters of privacy it is the chronicler's business to deal, and indeed they are often approached far more nearly than is necessary. We merely wish, without needless amplification, to indicate the standpoint of an earlier George Sand who was very quick to attach and also to detach herself—staking her all on a passion and losing it like a reckless gambler; being each time cured of her passion, though not of the venture itself; bringing to these various trials an incorrigible simplicity and an easy good-nature; joining to her successive adorations incidental cults for different arts and sciences—poetry with one, music with another, philosophy with a third. This is she whose image is engraved on the minds of her contemporaries in the heyday of her youth and earliest triumphs—she who, in meanly garb, lived now as a student or artist, now as a pilgrim, in the Quartier-Latin and on all the highways of Europe, particularly on the thoroughfares of Bohemia and other imaginary countries, braving the chances of a good or bad lodging, accepting the comradeship of any travellers she might meet—for a moment illuminating their personality by the fire of her imagination, and sharing or receiving their wild hospitality, their strange fancies, their irremediable passions. Heine, who often saw her towards the end of this period (1833-1840), has left us a vivid sketch of her which must be faithful. "Her face might perhaps be called more beautiful than interesting," he says; "yet the cast of her features is not severely antique, as it is softened by modern sentiment, which enwraps them with a veil of sadness. Her forehead is not high, and a wealth of hair of a most beautiful auburn colour falls on either side her head to her shoulders. Her nose is not aquiline and decided, nor is it an intelligent little snub-nose. It is simply a straight and ordinary one. A most good-humoured though not very attractive smile generally plays around her mouth; her lower lip, which is slightly inclined to droop, seems to betray fatigue. Her chin is plump, but of very beautiful form. So are her shoulders, which are magnificent. . . . Her voice is dull and muffled, with no sonorous tones, but it is sweet and pleasant. . . . Her conversation is not brilliant. She has absolutely none of the sparkling wit that distinguishes her countrywomen; neither has she their inexhaustible power of chattering. She listens to the conversation of others with a pleasant and sometimes singular smile, as if she were trying to absorb their best utterances. . . . M. de Musset one day called my attention to this peculiarity: '*It gives her a great advantage over us*,' he said."* And the sketch is quietly continued in the same moderate tone, enlivened here and there by some of those epigrams from which the author could not long abstain.

There seems no reason to linger over this first portrait. The second part of this life, which is also much the longer part, has special interest for us because she organises and governs it by her own unfettered will, "sheltering it as far as possible from the accidents of events or the caprices of affection." Let us follow her, when she finally leaves the life of adventure and the wandering, homeless existence, into the retirement of

* Lutèce.

Nohant—the relics and remembrances of which she has so dearly bought—where she gathers her children, sees them grow up, marries them; where, later on, the heart of the young grandmother, in its deep, calm joy, will go out to the grandchildren without for an instant interfering with the incessant productiveness, or checking the prodigality of the brain which has filled nearly half a century with its dreams and inventions, its ideas and its passions, which has charmed or startled and stirred the soul of five or six generations. For we should note that silence, which is one form of forgetfulness, did not begin for her until after her death. As long as she lived she wrote, and powerfully acted on the minds of her contemporaries; for it surely is acting, thus to agitate the minds of one's time, to disquiet consciences, to produce those great movements of sympathy or antipathy which are the ebb and flow of public opinion. And who in the present century has done this more than George Sand?

She has drawn herself, almost unconsciously, in this second part of her life in her *Correspondence*, which is much more instructive here than the *Histoire de ma Vie*, as that stops abruptly at the most splendid moment of her literary career. It is the *Correspondence*, particularly the very rich portion extending over the last five-and-twenty years, to which we turn to compare the author's impressions with our own remembrances—those brought away from a visit paid to Nohant in the June of 1861.

About this time, which already seems so distant, George Sand was writing to beg one of her friends to come and see her: "We still have beautiful days here. Our climate is clearer and warmer than that of the neighbourhood of Paris. The country is not generally fine: the soil calcareous, very *frumental*, but little conducive to the development of large trees; soft harmonious lines, many but small trees, an immense air of solitude—these are all its merits. You must prepare yourself to find my country like myself—of insignificant aspect. It has its good points when one knows it, but it is scarcely more opulent and demonstrative than its inhabitants.

Undemonstrative—that was true, as Heine had formerly pointed out; even insignificant of stature—why should I not say it?—that was also true according to my first impression of her. At the time of our meeting her fifty-seven years had left their inevitable mark—deadening the effect of her individuality, extinguishing the youthful and impassioned grace of former times, as well as the play of countenance which, as it lighted up the heaviness of certain features, had been her chief beauty. The figure had thickened, the eyes, though still beautiful, were obscured in an indescribable vagueness or indolence, which had increased with age. All this gave one the impression of a slight inertness and intellectual fatigue; it seemed as if her first impulse was to turn away from new lights, or the communcation of new ideas, which did not at once coincide with her own, or responded to them with difficulty.

She was hospitable, but gravely and silently so; and if one had held to one's first impression of her, she might have been rather severely judged: it was necessary to get rid of this impression, and then one found, according to her own saying, that she and her country had good points on a nearer acquaintance. It may perhaps be thought that this first coldness was accidental, and intended for the unexpected guest of 1861. This would be a natural, but it is not an accurate conclusion. There is a very delightful story touching the arrival at Nohant of an eagerly expected and longed-for guest, Théophile Gautier, and his impressions thereupon. He had, for her sake, made the great sacrifice of leaving his *boulevard*, and he did so with the Parisian's conviction that he was a hero in going to see a friend in the country; he reached Nohant in the full persuasion of his heroism and in the expectation of being rewarded by George Sand's great joy—looking for a welcome proportioned to the eagerness, if not vehemence, of the invitation. However, George Sand shows the greatest calmness, nay, she is more than calm, she is silent, and assumes the indolent, wearied air which had struck me. She leaves him for a moment to give some orders. He, astonished and increasingly displeased, bitterly complains of this reception to his travelling companion (a frequenter of the house); his displeasure, as is always the case, rises as he expresses it —he declares he will go, and collects his hat, stick, and bag. The witness of this wrath goes in the utmost haste to warn George Sand, so that she may avert it. At first she cannot understand the situation, but as its meaning dawns upon her, she shudders at the idea of such a calamity; the mistake upsets her completely, and she abandons herself to despair. "Then you cannot have told him *that I was an idiot?*" she ingenuously exclaims. She is hurried back to Théophile Gautier; explanations ensue, and soon happily end; he perceives by her accent of despair how much he was mistaken, and the re-entrance is a triumph.

George Sand's conversation was strictly to the point. She had never been talkative, and with advancing years became still less so, except when she was taking part in the family games or amusing the children with her stories. Of wit she had none, either in the Parisian or in the Gallic sense of the word. She admired it inordinately in others, though she had some difficulty in understanding it: to follow the play of wit and to accustom herself to the surprise which it always gave her, required on her part a decided effort of attention. Left to herself, she would have held aloof from these startling fancies and lively sallies, the attack and the retort, the brisk gymnastic exercise of the idea in which many of her friends and contemporaries excelled; indeed, she would have made but a sorry figure among them if they had not been well aware of her supreme mental power. I cannot easily imagine her at the famous dinners at Magny's, which at that time were a rallying-point for the most brilliant tilters with pen or word. She used herself to fear that her presence (for she went whenever she happened to be passing through Paris) was a cause of embarrassment to the others, and induced constraint in the dazzling paradoxical conversation which always roused her wonder. "Thanks to you," she writes to one of her most indefatigable correspondents, "I have as clear an idea of the *dîner Magny* as if I had been there. Only I think that it must have been more lively without me, as Théo* is occasionally seized with remorse when he has been too audacious for my taste. But Heaven knows that I would not damp his vivacity for anything in the world. It so well sets off the unchanging gentleness of the adorable Renan with the head of *Charles the Wise*." It is certainly difficult to fancy George Sand in her calm earnestness holding her own against the terrible raillery of Sainte-Beuve, the leader of the choir, the irony of Flaubert, the "exuberant" paradoxes of Théophile Gautier. She would sometimes express her disapproval of this excess of wit, and what she called *la blague* and pretension (a word which occurs very frequently in her correspondence), in the Parisian artists and literary men. She feels she must protest in the name of good-sense, good-taste, and the earnestness of life when the bounds have been passed. "I do not know," she says in a letter to Flaubert, "whether you were at Magny's one day when I told them that they were all *gentlemen*. They said that one ought not to write for the ignorant, and they laughed me to scorn because I would write for them exclusively, as they alone need anything. The learned are well provided for, they are rich and satisfied.

* Théophile Gautier.

The fools want everything, and I pity them. Love and pity cannot be separated. Here you have the very simple mechanism of my thought." She converted no one in speaking thus, but she gave everyone an additional reason for respecting her.

This was the light in which she appeared to me on the day we spent together. There were many important differences between us; but among the celebrated authors I have known (and even among those who are not celebrated) I have never met one who more sincerely respected the opinions of others or was less wishful to obtrude his own ideas. She put her adversaries at ease by a good-humoured tone in which there was not the least affectation; she would express her views in a simple, sober way, and then put them aside. Even in her letters she did not like discussions, and never willingly prolonged them—at least as concerned her social and political ideas; for though her whole soul was in them, she feared to compromise them by entering into controversy. "I have not the faculty of discussion," she said, "and I fly from all disputes; because I should always be beaten even if I were right ten thousand times over." And, when, for once, she does venture to approach the burning question of her humanitarian dreams, she cuts short the discussion as soon as possible: "It seems that I am not clear in my discourses, so that I have something in common with the orthodox, though I do not belong to them: I have no settled convictions either upon equality or authority. You appear to think that I wish to convert you to some doctrine:—on the contrary, it does not even occur to me to try. Everyone sees from his own point of view, and I respect his choice of it. I can give you mine in very few words: 'Not to take up one's position behind the opaque glass in which one can only see the reflection of one's own nose.'"

The *insignificance of aspect* disappeared after the first look. If chance or a happy inspiration led the conversation to certain subjects which were familiar to her, the cold and sluggish language became animated, the great, languid eyes would brighten into life and fire. There were two subjects especially on which she liked to converse: home-life and the drama. It was not easy to draw her to speak of the novel, even of her own novels. It is a remarkable fact that she would almost entirely forget them, and there was no affectation in this—it was simply a form or a sign of the natural genius which worked in her almost independently of any effort of her will. Succeeding years would bring other inspirations, and these banished the former ones. She is therefore perfectly sincere when she says, in her letters, that she is renewing her acquaintance with her most celebrated novels. They are literally new to her. What she told me of the singular sensations of an author who is recovering his own identity, is repeated—and most happily expressed—in a letter written about the same time to Dumas *fils*: "Every ten or fifteen years I devote myself to this study, in which I am as impartial as if it did not concern me in the least; for I even forget the names of the characters, only remembering the subject, but nothing whatever of the means of its elaboration. I am very far from being satisfied with the result of my study. I have now re-read *l'Homme de Neige* and *le Château des Désertes.* What I think of them is not of much consequence; but the phenomenon which I sought and have found is curious enough, and may be useful to you." She had at that time fallen into the temporary state of sterility from which every author suffers. Still it was necessary to make an effort. "But then, your humble servant is not there! George Sand is as far from himself as if he had passed into a state of fossilisation. At first there is no trace of an idea; then, when the ideas return there is no means of expressing them." In absolute despair she turned to one or two of her own novels. Still, nothing was clear to her. "Light gradually dawns: I recognise myself, I see my strong and weak points, and I regain possession of my literary being. So this is done with for the present, and I need not read myself again for a long time."

She was peculiarly modest: a *man* of letters without the characteristic defect of being absorbed in herself and her works. She was keenly alive to praise, and certainly recognised her own superiority; but it was the gift of production that she esteemed, rather than any particular work. Without help she could never recall the name of any of her novels; and if some name did half come back to her mind, her remembrance of it would be most confused and vague. I have rarely seen such complete indifference in an author; and I astonished her several times by the faithfulness of my memory, which was more grateful than her own for so many delightful and impassioned works.

In reality (and I scarcely dare to say this, so much is the word decried by the school of refined artists) she was a *bourgeoise;* she was distinctly of the respectable middle-class. She had the habits and the instincts of a woman of that class, especially the instinct of motherhood, to which she seemed predestined; though that instinct was often falsified and diverted from its end. It was a *bourgeoise* nature with a Byronic imagination. Her letters are full of allusions to her home-cares, her anxieties about her children, her housekeeping. All hinges upon this; she is continually begging her friends to come and see where she has taken root. Different indeed is she, in this last period of her life, from the superb and fantastic Amazon who, in her mad freaks, rode rough-shod over broken hearts! But this is the same being restored to fairly normal conditions of existence: from the midst of her family circle she will describe the life which has become her dearest necessity and, as it were, her last religion. "There is always the same monastic regularity at Nohant—breakfast, the walking-hours, the five hours of work for those who do work, dinner, the game of dominoes, fancy-work while Manceau* reads me a novel; Nini† sitting on the table and working too; our friend Borie snoring with his face

* A young engraver in bad health, who was her guest.

† One of her grandchildren.

over the stove and pretending that he is not asleep at all; Solange teasing him; Émile (Aucante) delivering himself of set phrases." Here is the family group, to which a few friendly faces are added; for this Nohant is a hospitable inn, a Scotch hostelry, open to friends all the year round. In the day-time, when she is well, she works in her little Trianon; she gathers up stones in her wheel-barrow, weeds, plants ivy; she exhausts herself in a doll's garden—it makes her sleep, she says, and gives her the best of appetites. One can see her still—and in what a grotesque costume did I surprise this good cultivator of the soil!

And she had sought such a home-life in the most adverse circumstances, though always on condition that she was allowed a certain liberty which is not usually compatible with it. What was her predominant feeling when she established herself in Majorca with her children, carrying in her train the poor, suffering Chopin? Her letters of the winter of 1839—written from the Abbey of Valdemosa—must be read to understand how all her affections had been absorbed in one passionate feeling—the feeling of motherhood; and this she extended to the invalid, the great artist. In this oddly assorted family is he not like another child which commands her care and devotion? May there not have been some mistake here? The old Carthusian monastery was full of poetry, the scenery was wonderful in its wildness and grandeur, eagles soared in the sky above; but the climate became terrible, rain descended in torrents, and the hostile inhabitants shunned them as if they had been infected with the plague. Still all this could have been endured if Chopin had been able to bear it; but his lungs were mortally affected, and he grew rapidly worse. A maid, brought from France at a great expense, refused to fulfil her duties, which she considered too hard. The time came when Lélia herself could bear no more. After having swept and cooked she too was worn out with fatigue; and besides this labour, she had the teaching of Maurice and Solange, her literary work and the constant attendance on the invalid, whose condition caused her terrible anxiety. At last—must we say it?—Lélia fell a prey to rheumatism. They left the island, and, thanks to her, Chopin was able to leave too, and to reach Paris.* It was quite time. Without enlarging on this subject, we may say that the foundation of George Sand's most opposite attachments was nearly always a mysterious, vague, maternal instinct, which once called forth the apt remark that "she was the daughter of Jean-Jacques Rousseau and Madame de Warens." It was the moral weakness of this incomplete and lavish nature which caused the attempt to reconcile irreconcilable feelings in a way that opinion, and even the most indulgent opinion, pronounced equivocal, and refused to understand.

When the maternal instinct had been nearly purified

* See, particularly, the letters of November 14th and December 14th, 1838, and those of January 15th and 20th, February 22nd and March 8th, 1839.

rom all alloy and restored to its real objects, it took absolute, almost tyrannical possession of her life. Family life becomes all in all. She is the slave of her children and grandchildren; her whole existence is devoted to keeping them happy with toys and stories, educating them, and later, providing them with marriage-portions and seeking advantageous alliances for them. It is for them that she founds her famous theatre of marionnettes, which holds so large a place in her life. Maurice is the *impresario;* herself the poet of the little dramas.* "I am very lively still, and though I cannot produce for the amusement of others, I can help in their amusements."

When, after an interval in the garden—not far from the river where, in a fit of youthful despair, she had once tried to end a life whose future already troubled her—she consented to take me over the house, it was to the little theatre that she led me first, as to a place consecrated by joyous family rites. But it was empty and unfurnished. On its damp walls I could still see

"Du spectacle d'hier l'affiche déchirée."

There was a sense of temporary desertion in the pretty room, used to the applause and laughter of the

* Madame Sand carefully collected her chief plays in a single volume, *Le Théâtre de Nohant*, in which *le Drac*, *Plutus*, *le Pavé*, *la Nuit de Noël*, and *Marielle* may be found. These pieces are not here given exactly as they were produced on the Nohant stage, but as the author remembered them—writing them after their production.

family and of friends. The winter had been spent at Tamaris, near Toulon, on the shores of the Mediterranean. The return to Nohant was a little desolate and bewildering: the ordinary life was still in abeyance. As yet the mistress of the house did not know "where to bestow her person, and her old books and papers." A study was being arranged for her. Maurice had grown tired, during his stay at Tamaris, "of always seeing the sea and never crossing it," and he had taken flight to Africa. From thence he had gone to Cadiz and Lisbon in Prince Napoleon's yacht: there was even some idea of his going to America. It was holiday-time for the usual staff of actors at Nohant, and I believe I am right in saying that the great marionnette *Balandard*, so often alluded to in her letters, was under repair.

When one was at Nohant it was difficult to escape the gentle mania which possessed the whole house. I only escaped because the chief performers in the illustrious theatre were absent. Usually George Sand devoted herself to it heart and soul, and did wonders with her fairy-fingers. She arranged the *scenarii* and made the theatrical costumes; she sought new effects of word and illusion; she was unfeignedly enthusiastic about those which her son Maurice found. It was her fairy-land where she was artlessly happy; not thinking that there could be a greater pleasure for the friends whom she invited than this.* There is no doubt that her literary vocation for

* See a letter to Flaubert (December 31st, 1867), which is very interesting from this point of view.

the drama—which is, indeed, questionable—was produced and developed by her devotion to her puppets.

During several consecutive winters in the retreat of Nohant, she, with her children and a few friends, had found their principal amusement and occupation in these representations, to the thought and preparation of which whole days were sometimes given. This was a source of great astonishment to the immediate neighbours and the peasants, who were perplexed by the aimless excitement. Madame Sand has most vividly sketched this double life—the real and the artistic life—to which she gives a wider scene of action in one of her most interesting novelettes. The central idea is exactly the same. It is "a kind of mystery which was a natural consequence of the uproar prolonged far into the nights in the country, when the house was enveloped in snow and fog, when even the servants, who did not help in the changes of scene or in the suppers, had left the house at an early hour; the thunder, the pistol-shots, the beating of drums, the sounds of the drama and the ballet-music—all this was very weird, and the rare passers-by who heard something of it from afar did not hesitate to pronounce us either mad or bewitched." This is the idea from which this ingenious and charming story springs; it supplies a theme for the analysis of some artistic ideas; and it is not difficult to recognise in *le Château des Désertes* an idealised Nohant, and in Celio and Stella the children of those who had taken pleasure in representing some of her own characteristics in the touching portrait of Lucrezia Floriani. Thus in that skilful handling reality becomes art, often noble art. We should note in another novel, *l'Homme de Neige*, one of George Sand's most dramatic works, the important use which she makes of a puppet-show. It is somewhat like the introduction of the play in *Hamlet*—on a smaller scale, of course, and a more insignificant stage. But the scene itself is as essential as it is with Shakespeare; the greatest interests, the revelation and punishment of a crime which is suspected but not yet known, hang upon the performance which Christian Waldo and the lawyer Socflé give, putting their whole soul into the combination of the by-play and impromptu dialogue whence the *dénouement* is to issue. Another dramatised reminiscence of the *Théâtre de Nohant*.

A devoted mother, entirely absorbed in the family-life which she created around her, she liked to be presented in this aspect: and to this end she answered the questions of M. Louis Ulbach, who wished to give her portrait in a serial. She assured him that for five-and-twenty years her life had been very commonplace. "What would you have?" she says. "I cannot raise myself. I am only a good sort of woman to whom ferocious characteristics, which are entirely imaginary, are ascribed." She was very anxious that the public mind should be disabused of the legend of former times. "I have been accused of never having been capable of passionate love. It seems to me that my life has been given to tenderness, and that this might have sufficed.

Now, thank God, no one asks more of me: and those who are kind enough to love me, notwithstanding the lack of brilliancy in my life and mind, do not complain of me."

She said much the same to me in very simple language. It seems to me that in abridging this biographical letter I reproduce some of her conversational peculiarities. She tells us that she wrote easily and with pleasure; it was her recreation. Her correspondence was enormous, and that was work indeed. If one only had to write to one's friends! but she was assailed with letters. "What ridiculous or touching requests come to me! I do not answer them when I can do nothing. Some of these deserve to be furthered even when there is little hope of success. Then one must say that one will try . . . . I hope after my death to go to a planet where reading and writing are not known." Everyone has his own idea of Paradise. She had written so much during her life that she wanted all Eternity to rest in. And in fact she was kindness itself, though her kindness was never foolish. On glancing through this vast correspondence, it is impossible not to be touched with the benevolence, or rather the charity of soul and art which this superior woman shows in adapting herself to all who implore her aid, howsoever small their talent; in the ungrudging praise that encourages some, in the cautious sincerity intended to discourage others. The political advocate in her is especially indefatigable. More liberal than her party, although, as she tells us, she is a republican by birth, she is never weary of asking—not for herself, indeed! but for friends or political clients who were threatened or proscribed after the *Coup d'État*, begging that they may be allowed to remain in France, or that they may be recalled from exile—and from whom? from Prince Louis Napoleon himself, President first and afterwards Emperor, who allowed her almost unlimited credit in influence. George Sand did not temporise; without in the least altering her opinion she nearly always obtained what she asked for, and this does the greatest honour both to the asker and the asked. It is one of the rare instances in which the rights of humanity have been able to conquer the pride of irreconcilable parties and that of absolute power.

George Sand concealed nothing, or scarcely anything of her private affairs. The strict regularity of her life was only modified by a few excursions in France which were necessary to the scenery of her novels. I do not include here a sojourn at Palaiseau towards the end of her life, to bring her, as she said, within reach of the Paris theatres, where several of her plays were about to be produced. With the exception of this short interval she remained at Nohant. She wished to die there; and did so, in fact, at the age of seventy-two, on the 8th February, 1876. There was no reason that she should have been reticent on her pecuniary affairs: "My accounts are not confused. I have certainly made a million by my work (this is in 1869); I have not put by a *sou*: all is given away except twenty thousand francs, which I have invested, that my *tisane* may not cost my children too much if I should be ill. And indeed I am not very sure of being able to reserve this capital; for there is sure to be some one in need of it, and if I am well enough to renew it, my economies will assuredly be relaxed. Therefore keep my secret, that I may be economical as long as possible."

When she made any allusion to some event in her past life she had a way of absorbing herself without concealing anything which had a quaintly good-humoured effect. "I no doubt have grave faults, but I am like the rest of the world, and do not see them. Neither do I know whether I have talents or virtues. If one has done right one does not praise oneself, one simply thinks oneself logical. If one has done wrong, it was from ignorance. With more light one would never do wrong again." This examination of conscience may be considered too lax and comfortable. I give it as it is and for what it is worth—an ingenuous declaration that she has a large indulgence for others, and thinks it only just that she should profit by it herself; then she playfully adds: "You wish to know more than there is to know . . . . The individual called George Sand gathers flowers, classifies her plants, makes dresses and mantles for her little world and costumes for the marionettes, reads music, and, above all, spends hours with her grandchildren . . . . She has not always been so satisfactory. There was a time when she was foolish enough to be young; but as she did no harm, as she was innocent of evil passions and did not live for vanity, she is happy enough to be peaceful now and to be able to enjoy everything."

When I met her at Nohant she had just come back laden with plants gathered on the shores of the Mediterranean and in Savoy. She was dreading the classification of these plants, and indeed, while talking, the whole day was given up to that work. But there were other and different arrangements to be made in the house. Her study was a sorry sight—it was depressing even to glance round it. Another was being prepared in which George Sand thought she should work very pleasantly; and in the meantime her study was her bedroom. She showed me on a very plain table a pile of large sheets of blue paper, ready cut in quarto size. "When you go, this evening," she said, "I shall set to work; and I shall not go to bed until I have filled twelve of these pages." It was her daily task. Her work was regulated thus: she counted on the punctuality of the inspiration, which rarely failed her.

For me, this was an almost unlooked-for occasion of becoming acquainted with her method of work, the results of which had always astonished me—not only by their abundance, but by their exact regularity. At this period of her life the least she produced every year was "her little novel" and a dramatic piece. "I am only an old retired troubadour who occasionally sings his ditty to the moon; not caring much whether he sings well or badly, provided that he expresses the theme which runs in his head, the rest of the time idling delightfully."

I had carefully studied her work, and two points in it especially struck me: the marvellous facility of her talent, which almost savoured of carelessness, and the too plainly visible absence of composition in her best works. As I gave her my impressions she clearly perceived that I made reserves even in the purely literary view of the subject, and quite independently of any vital question. She became dissatisfied—not because I made some re-reserves, but because I kept them to myseif—and begged me to be entirely open with her. I therefore explained myself fully on these two points, as I was bound to do. She thanked me, and applied the criticism much more severely than I had done myself, which gave me a very favourable opinion of her literary nature as being eager for truth and strong enough to resist the contemptible temptations of flattery. By recalling my impressions, and completing them with the numerous self-revelations contained in her most interesting letters, I have been able to form a fairly exact idea of her method of work, and her ideas on the conditions and requirements of her art; although these were merely instructive with her until the day of a celebrated discussion, when she was obliged to give them clear expression and definitive form.

It seems, indeed, that it was the pleasure of writing which impelled her, almost unthinkingly (and somewhat confusedly) to throw on paper in concrete and living form her dreams, her tenderness, her meditations, and her chimeras.

To account for this almost inconceivable facility in writing, one must remember that to the natural gift, that nothing can replace, she joined the treasure of experience and acquired knowledge which multiplies the resources of talent and allows of its being varied—not without fatiguing it, perhaps, but certainly without exhausting it. The gift of nature verifies, but hardly analyses itself. How is it possible to explain this phenomenon of an imagination which falls passionately in love with its own creations, of a faculty of expression which suddenly presents itself, quite ready, without having been prepared, which adapts itself almost without hesitation or effort to the most diverse subjects, to analysis and action—as if the author found nothing so easy and natural as to relate the visions of her soul, and show to others the characters and dramas at work within her by means of a style which is simply her thought made visible? That is the gift, it exists, and one does meet these predestined spirits who sport with expression, luminous ease, and graceful liberty; while other writers, profound but laborious artists, torment themselves and weary their intellect in accomplishing their work, achieving success indeed, but at the cost of an effort which is perceptible in every page, in every sentence, in every word. The ground is deeply ploughed, but the reader feels as if he had been helping in the work himself, hence—according to the writer's stand-point—that esteem or admiration which is not unmixed with a sensation of fatigue.

But in George Sand the natural gift is joined to great and varied culture. She had read much, though unmethodically; but her diverse studies had left behind a rich alluvium which combined with her own resources and wonderfully enriched and assisted her fertility. No one has better understood or expressed the necessity of study in art. "I know nothing," she said; "still I possess something from having read much and learnt much . . . . I know nothing because my memory is gone; but I have learnt a great deal, and when I was seventeen I used to spend my nights in study. If these things are not distinctly present with me, they have nevertheless left their honey in my mind." We have indeed seen in the *Histoire de ma Vie* the extent and impulsiveness of her reading; but it had not been sterile, since from each author, poet, philosopher, publicist—Byron, Goethe, Leibnitz, Rousseau—she had retained some particle which revolved rather confusedly in the vast and powerful current of the cerebral life. She was never tired of recommending this method to the *dilettanti*, the amateurs, and also the young idlers who addressed themselves to her as to an accommodating adviser, expecting her to say, "You have genius; trust to it, and go on fearlessly." This is the usual answer given by the great chamber-council of glory to all who importune them. In order to get rid of them they flatter them with some stereotyped compliment, and bestow on them their literary benediction. But George always abstained from paying young aspirants to art with this species of base coin. "You wish, I know, to be a literary man," she writes to one of them. "I have told you that this is possible if you learn everything. Art is not a gift which can dispense with extensive knowledge in any sense of the word . . . . You may be struck with the want of solidity in the greater number of actual works and productions : it proceeds entirely from want of study. A mind is never satisfactorily formed if it has not conquered the difficulties of every kind of work, or such work at least as requires the tension of the will." With those in whom she is interested she is implacable as regards this preparatory hygiene of the will, which does not indeed lead to erudition in the strict sense of the word, but does develop a special aptitude in understanding that will serve when it is required and when the author desires it. Art thrown back upon itself devours and consumes itself. "You have artistic tastes and instincts," she says to a favoured suppliant for her criticism, "but you may prove to yourself at any moment that the purely artistic artist is impotent—that is to say, mediocre or excessive—that is to say, mad . . . . You think that you can produce without having amassed . . . . You think that one can manage with reflection and advice. No, one cannot do so. It is necessary to have lived and searched. It is necessary to have digested much ; to have loved and suffered and waited, and to be always labouring. In short, one must understand fencing before one handles a sword.

Do you wish to be like those literary whipper-snappers who think themselves fine fellows because they print platitude and trash? Fly from them as you would from the plague; they are the animalcules *(vibrions)* of literature."* One must acknowledge that this is proud and manly rhetoric, worth more than any rhetoric of schools. It was the powerful voice of a ripened genius; the counsel of her old age to the impatient youth of her petitioners, framed in the loftiest morality. "Art is a sacred thing," she exclaims, "a chalice which must not be approached without prayer and fasting. Forget it, if you cannot devote yourself at once to the study of essential things and the trial of the young provers of invention."

* In connection with these injunctions we would draw attention to others taken from some inedited letters to Count d'A——, whose daughter-in-law has since become one of our best novelists. Madame Sand insisted above all things on the importance of respecting the originality of each aspirant to the literary career. "You know," she says, "that I am entirely at your service. But believe me when I beg you not to submit the talent and future of your young writer to any opinion whatever, not even to mine. Let her venture and produce herself spontaneously. I know by experience that the most sincere advice may check the impulse and modify the individuality . . . She knows how to write, she is appreciative, she is quite capable of good criticism. As regards imagination, if she is devoid of it no advice will give it her; if not, it is very possible that advice may destroy it. Tell her that as long as I consulted others I was never inspired, but that inspiration came to me directly I ventured to walk alone." (August 6th, 1860.)

"The study of essential things"—that is the condition upon which the existence of the future author depends. If he has not beforehand amassed a treasure of serious knowledge, in such order as he may choose, of the ideas in which the great human curiosity has exercised itself—history, natural science, law, political economy, philosophy,—what good is the instrument to him? The instrument works in vacuity: what becomes of the artist in his frivolous labour if he does not apply it to some resisting substance, if he troubles himself only about the manner and is indifferent to the matter, if he does not make it an absolute rule to penetrate every subject beyond the point required by shallowness and conventionality, and to give foundation and solidity to his creation?

This is excellent advice: throughout her life she never failed to apply it to herself; she never ceased to exercise her mobile and enthusiastic curiosity in the most diverse forms of human knowledge. And if art must have roots as well as life, there were certainly roots, and ancient roots in hers, which she ceaselessly developed and strengthened in the soil whence her talent sprang in such superb luxuriance. She would be absorbed in some science such as that of natural history, which she had made her constant study, or in a wider sense in Nature, which she ever contemplated both with mental and bodily vision. She would absolutely lose herself in a problem of natural history, never abandoning it until it was solved: and while in search of the solution she was dead to all else. For instance, she and her son Maurice (who had developed a like passion) would be occupied for months together in researches of this nature, and at such times her brain was possessed by terms, more or less barbarous, to the exclusion of all beside. She saw nothing in her dreams but rhomboidal prisms, scintillating reflections, dim cleavages, cleavages full of rosin; they spent long hours in asking each other: "Have you grasped the *orthosis?* Do you hold the *albitès?*" The day after these scientific orgies she had the greatest difficulty in returning to ordinary life and her usual work, though in the end she returned to them in greater intensity. At other times she would be absorbed in botany: "What I should like best would be to give myself entirely up to it; that would be my paradise on earth." And were not her yearly tours in France a study of the same kind? "I like to have seen what I describe. If I have only three words to say about a place I like to be able to see it in my memory, and make as few mistakes as possible." She had a way of silently observing nature which was peculiar to herself. But it was an active silence; she absorbed every detail in a scene before her, and brought it, living, to her spiritual vision, as clear as perception itself. Hence the truth and charm of her landscapes. Even when we have not seen them with our bodily eyes, we involuntarily exclaim as at the portrait by a great master, the original of which is not known to us, "How exactly like!" The power of the art makes one believe in the resemblance.

There were other and deeper roots which had attached her from early youth to certain philosophical, political, and religious ideas.* They had penetrated deeply into that eager, open soul at a very early period, and had been exaggerated and perverted at a very early period also. In the course of time, however, some were modified by the natural force of a healthy mind; others relaxed their former rigidity in the rude school of life. Rather than again insist on the aberrations of taste and good-sense, which had exposed George Sand to the anxieties of the public conscience, and even to the hatred and vengeance of the two diametrically opposite sides of opinion—the side of Proudhon and that of Louis Veuillot —I would show her in the last period of her life, not as a convert to moderation or as a fugitive from her former ideas, but as applying herself with praiseworthy sincerity to their modification in a degree more acceptable to herself, and as reconquering, on certain points at least, the liberty of her *ego* and the independence of her mind.

There is, indeed, still a considerable proportion of exaggeration and paradox in her ideas. But how far

* "What she tolerated least was the opinion of certain shallow critics who say 'that it is not necessary in writing to have a belief of one's own; that it is quite sufficient if one reflects facts and figures like a mirror . . . .' No, this is not true; the reader attaches himself to the writer only so far as the writer has individuality, whether it pleases or shocks him. He feels that he has to do with a living soul, not with an instrument." (March 1st, 1863, *Correspondance Inédite*, mentioned above.)

she is, both in time and opinion, from the rebel of other days! Since the experience of the war and the Commune, it is only by slight touches here and there in her correspondence that one can recognise the former friend of Mazzini and Armand Barbès, the Utopist of the reforms in the position of women and of marriage, the enthusiastic disciple of the gospel of Pierre Leroux, the sectary of Christianity as reformed by the gloomy pantheism of Lamennais, and later, the ardent revolutionist of 1848, the collaborator of Ledru-Rollin, the menacing editor of the *Bulletins de la République*, which emanated from the *Ministère de l'Intérieur*. All these events in politics and social philosophy were not lost upon her. We will not seek to prove this at length. I will not even take my proofs from the famous *Journal d'un Voyageur pendant la Guerre*, which had such success in the *Revue des Deux Mondes*, to the horror of some of its readers, but from the Correspondence itself, a witness that cannot misrepresent. On April 28th, 1871, she wrote to Flaubert: "The experiment which Paris is trying or undergoing proves nothing against the laws of progress, and if I have some principles, good or bad, laid up in my mind, they are neither shaken nor modified by it. I have long accepted patience as one accepts the weather, the duration of winter, old age, failure in all its forms. But I think that (sincere) partisans should change their formula, or rather, perhaps, perceive the emptiness of any *a priori* formula." And to Madame Adam, on June 4th of the same year: "Let us shed tears of blood over our illusions and our errors . . . . Our principles may and ought to remain the same, but the application becomes more difficult; and it may be that we shall find ourselves condemned to will what we do not desire."

Notwithstanding these assertions the principles were practically modified, though their substance might not have changed. To a young enthusiast who sent her a political poem she wrote: "Thank you; but do not dedicate those verses to me . . . . I hate bloodshed, and I want no more of that argument: 'let us do evil that good may come; let us kill that we may create.' No, no, my old age protests against the tolerance in which my youth floated. We must get rid of the theories of 1793; they have ruined us. Reign of Terror and Massacre of St. Bartholomew—it is the same direction. Curse all who dig *charnel-houses*. Life does not proceed from thence. It is an historical error of which we must be disabused; evil engenders evil. . . ." (October 21st, 1871.) And in the familiar style for which she has almost too great a fancy, and with the *tutoiement* that in her is a lingering habit of the artist-life, she says to Flaubert: "I have written day by day my impressions and reflections during the crisis. The *Revue des Deux Mondes* publishes that journal. If you read it you will see that the very foundations of life have been shaken everywhere, even in places which the war has not reached! You will also see that though I am very gullible I have not swallowed the humbug of parties." The style is not lofty, but how expressive it is!

She laughs at the blind and confiding enthusiasm of her past life, that optimism which would not brook delay, but desired immediate progress at any cost, were it even by means of force. Still she had done much towards amending her nature: and now the events in Paris stir up all the old questions again! "I was beginning to get the upper hand of my own character, I had extinguished vain ebullitions, I had sown grass and flowers on my volcanoes, and they were thriving well. I was beginning to imagine that the whole world might be enlightened, corrected, or restrained . . . . and now I wake from a dream. . . . However it is not good to despair. . . . It will pass, I hope. But *I am suffering from the sickness of my nation and my race.*" "Let us not allow ourselves to die!" she continually exclaims; adding: "I speak as if I expected to live indefinitely; I forget that I am very old. What matter? I shall live in those who survive me." (1871.)

On all points, even in the region of philosophy, this remarkable tranquillisation is apparent; the excessive passion which kindled a lurid flame in every idea is stilled. She remains, indeed, the ardent spiritualist she has always been, but she does not now think herself obliged to do battle with Christianity; she no longer fulminates, she is neutral. We should look in vain, in the correspondence of the last years of her life, for those previous denunciations of the priest which broke forth, both in season and out of season, in her letters and novels twenty years earlier. As to her philosophical convictions, she defends them with indomitable and praiseworthy obstinacy against the opposite intolerance of the materialism that claims to be scientific. She will not submit to be told to "believe this, or you are behind the age; let us destroy that we may prove, and pull down everything that we may reconstruct." She answers: "Confine yourselves to proving, and do not dictate to us." The work of science is not to overthrow with angry blows and with the aid of the passions . . . . you say that "either faith must burn and slay science, or science must hunt down and dissipate faith." This mutual extermination will not, in my opinion, be the result of one battle, or the work of one generation. "Liberty would perish in it."* She does not see the necessity of forcing her understanding to expel noble ideas and destroying certain faculties in herself *for the purpose of playing a trick upon the devout.* "It is not necessary or useful thus to persist in proclaiming nothingness; we are completely ignorant thereupon. I think that at present there is excessive zeal in advancing a narrow and somewhat coarse realism, both in science and in art."

One can see that she had gradually freed herself from the party bonds which had so strictly restrained her; she had also shaken off certain excessive influences which

* Letter to M. Louis Viardot, June 10th, 1868.

had considerably affected her individuality. And she is restored to herself, she takes possession of herself, with her convictions and her chimeras too, indeed—but at least they are her own, and constitute her *ego*. She remounts to a level from which her own passion, still more that of others, had too often dragged her down.

In the interval much fresh talent had appeared. As regarded her personal work at least, she was desirous of becoming thoroughly conversant with each new author. She was vividly interested in these different manifestations of the literary life. She was for some time on terms of exquisite courtesy with Octave Feuillet, whom she commended warmly and spontaneously for the *Roman d'un Jeune Homme Pauvre;* this cordiality continued until the appearance of the *Histoire de Sibylle*, which provoked a bitter and passionate answer from her—*Mademoiselle de La Quintinie.* The beginning of Edmond About's career was watched by her with much interest; she gave her approbation—though not without some protest against the system of perpetual raillery. "We were considerably ridiculed for our eternal despair thirty years ago. You laugh in the present day; but you laugh much more sadly than we wept." She was continually and perpetually astonished that the young authors should persist "in seeing and in showing life only in such a light as painfully disgusts all one's better feelings. We endeavoured to portray suffering man, the victim of life. You portray the ardent man who resists suffering, but who, instead of flinging away the cup, re-fills it to the brim and drinks it to the dregs. But this cup of strength and life kills you; as is proved by the fact that all the characters in *Madelon* are dead at the close of the drama, shamefully dead, except *Elle*, the personification of vice, who is still young and triumphant. "This spirit of bias in success, if not in sympathy, irritates her. "What, then, is your conclusion? Is this vice alone a power, is there no force in honour and virtue? . . . I agree with you that Feuillet and myself, each from his own point of view, produce legends rather than novels of manners. I only ask you to do what we cannot do; and as you have such accurate knowledge of the wounds and the leprosy of this society, to raise up their *sense of strength* in the region which you represent so truly."* Alexandre Dumas was simply worshipped by her with a worship composed of admiration and tenderness. She rejoices intensely in his success; she reads *l'Affaire Clémenceau* with maternal a solicitude which immediately suggests the rejoinder to him—which later, and with a difference of sex, may possibly be seen in *la Princesse Georges*. When, after the war and the Commune, Alexandre Dumas becomes for the moment a publicist, and borrows Junius's mask and pen, her applause is rapturous; she proclaims it to be simply a masterpiece. "How you go to the bottom of everything, and how well you know how to give facts, where I only give intentions! And then how well it is said! you are at once terse and

* Letter to M. Edmond About, March, 1863.

ample, vigorous, pathetic, and solid!" She was never weary of admiring the understanding of scenic force, the *vis dramatica*, which she was very proud of having divined: "Do you remember my telling you, after *Diane de Lys*, that you would outlive them all? . . . I remember it, because my impression was so strong, so absolutely certain. You seemed not to suspect it, you were so young! Perhaps I revealed you to yourself; and if so, there is one good thing that I have done in my life."

She had felt so much anxiety in transforming her novels into plays, not professing, besides, great art in scenic arrangement, that she was struck by the unconstrained manner and strong evidence of truth in situations and feelings where *others* did not escape being conventional. "And how much progress you have made since that time! You now know what you are doing, and how to lead the public. You will make further and ceaseless progress."* The public must say whether this kindly prophecy, which she sent him with her maternal benediction, has been realised.

If I wished to define the character of George Sand's mind irrespectively of the episodes and adventures of her literary life, I should say that it was dogmatic and impassioned. She was dogmatic in so far as she had strong convictions on fundamental subjects. One must distinguish faith in ideas from the intrinsic value of those

* Letter to Alexandre Dumas, May 23rd, 1871. For the beginning of this friendship, see the letter to M. Charles Edmond, November 27th, 1857.

ideas. Whatever the value of hers may have been, she believed in them firmly, she was deeply in earnest about them; and whatever the society in which she found herself she never allowed either sceptic or jester to turn them into ridicule. The best part of herself, her art, was instinctively subordinate to them. Now ideas have such force in themselves, that even if they are questionable they communicate something of that force to a mind that is nourished on them, and give it a tone of loftiness and generosity hardly to be found in those of which the æsthetics seem to be an absolute indifference. This is the secret of the superiority that George Sand seems to have maintained in her long correspondence with Flaubert, where some of the most delicate questions in literature were touched upon, and where also two artists, utterly different if not opposed in their conception of art, were able to control themselves reciprocally.

This amicable controversy lasted nearly twelve years, from 1864 to 1876. It is of little consequence how the literary friendship between two such different individualities began; they probably met each other at the famous *dîner Magny*, to which George Sand always went when she was in Paris, if only for the purpose of renewing her acquaintance with the world of letters which she forgot during the long months at Nohant. After this more or less fortuitous meeting, Flaubert had applauded with all his might at the first representation of *Villemer*, and George Sand in her gratitude wrote to him, saying that she "loved him with all her heart." The acquaintance established, the letters between them became increasingly frequent, and the correspondence lasted until George Sand's death. She had admired *Madame Bovary;* she at once detected the weak point in *Salammbô.* "It is a very fine and very powerful work," she said, "but it really has no interest except for artists and scholars. They question its merits all the more, but they read it; whereas the public contents itself with saying, 'It may be superb, but the people of that time do not interest me in the least.'"*

She had no doubt betrayed somewhat of this feeling in talking to Flaubert, who in his turn, it appears, had laughed at "the old troubadour of the inn time-piece, which always sings, and always will sing of perfect love." The name pleases George Sand; she merrily adopts it, and henceforth calls herself by it. The artist and the troubadour—here is the difference between the two authors characterised by two picturesque words which naturally suscitated the controversy. It is probable enough that before this period George Sand, although often cursorily touching in the subject of art, had never contemplated her own individual art, or clearly understood her method of composition and her aim. She had in this as in other things obeyed her instincts; still more the faculty of writing to relate and depict which in her expressed itself with such irresistible power and an ease that was simply inconceivable. She was led to reflect upon these subjects, and to

* Letter to Maurice Sand, June 20th, 1865.

define by herself the sight of the contrary tendencies and treasures of talent which arose on all sides; the comparison of the various forms of talent naturally forced itself upon her. Realism was only just beginning; she could scarcely have known of Zola's first and great success. But Flaubert, and Jules and Edmond de Goncourt revealed in all their works a new art, in which were combined the influence of Balzac in the intensity of observation, and that of Théophile Gautier in the anxiety and care for form. There were symptoms here which attracted the ever-wakeful and watchful curiosity of George Sand. She took advantage in the first place of the accidents of life, then of the friendship between herself and Flaubert, to define—as soon as she found herself able to do so—the differences of the literary temperament which she so strongly felt in presence of the new groups or individualities that best summarised the tendencies. There was a striking contrast between such a nature as hers—lavish to excess and with such a spontaneous and natural abundance in expression that she compares it herself to "the waters of a spring which flow without much idea of what they might reflect if they stopped," and a writer such as Flaubert—a laboriously, inventive, and expressive artist, as fastidious in regard to himself as he is in regard to others, anxious and dissatisfied in his work, one of the representatives of the group and race of excessive artists who are great labourers in form, jewellers in style, carvers of rare cameos, a wild hunter after the most expressive word or the most ornamental epithet, torturing himself as if the future of the world, or rather the future of art, depended upon one page, tormented by a species of morbid acuteness and subtlety in literary sensations—thus exhausting his rich artistic individuality in detail, indifferent to the vital meaning, taking no part or lot in the great ideas which lead the world, simply interested in noting the variety of characters which they inspire or the eccentricities which they produce, an impassible observer of the human puppets and the secret threads which guide them. It had not always been thus. In the history of this mind *Madame Bovary* represented an hour of dilatation and expansion, a richness and breadth in composition, a happiness in production, and a joy in fecundity which is not found in it later. That large vein was afterwards turned from the great human current to archæological curiosities or the peculiarities of pathological cases.

Hence a certain disaffection in the public and a growing unpopularity; hence, also, much umbrage and despondency in the author. George Sand does not weary in her efforts to raise him from these depths of discouragement; counsel flows freely and spontaneously from her heart and pen; she rouses and reassures him, scatters throughout the correspondence the soundest ideas on the true position of the artist—who ought not to isolate himself too proudly from humanity—on the conditions of art and on the duties that it imposes, which must not be confounded with the servitude and exaction extorted by cliques. In this part of the correspondence George Sand (though she is perfectly natural) takes up her position on a very high level both of mind and heart. Full of solicitude for the dear artist who is so sick and sorrowful, she makes the greatest efforts to communicate to him something of her own serenity and healthy vigour of mind. He must abandon himself more freely to his natural imagination, and torment it less, or he will paralyse it: "I am continually astonished by your laborious work; is it coquetry? . . . It is so little observable. . . . As to style, I hold it more cheaply than you do. The wind plays with my old harp as it pleases. It has its *heights* and its *depths*, its powerful and its weak notes; and really I do not much care, provided that the emotion comes—but I find nothing in *myself*. It is the *other* who sings at his pleasure, well or badly; and when I think about that I get frightened, and tell myself that I am nothing, nothing at all. A great wisdom saves us; we say to ourselves: 'Well, even if we are only instruments, still it is a delightful state of being, and there is no sensation like that of feeling oneself vibrate. . . .' Do let the wind play a little through your strings. I believe that you take more pains than is necessary, and that you should more often trust to the *other*. . . ." She constantly recurs to this recommendation, which contains in germ exactly the hygiene required by Flaubert, who has become the tormentor and the tormented of himself. "Be less cruel to yourself. Give yourself head-way; then, when the spirit has produced, you can raise the general tone and sacrifice what does not belong to the original plan. Is this impossible? I think not. What you do seems so easy and abundant, it is a perpetual overflow! I cannot understand this anguish." It pains her, too, to see that he gets angry with the public at every turn, that he cannot get rid of his wrath (*qu'il est indécolèreux*). At your age you should be less irritable, less taken up with the foolishness of others. In my own case I look upon it simply as lost time, as great a loss of time as it is to complain of the annoyance of rain or of flies. The public, which is so often told that it is stupid, grows angry, and becomes more stupid. After all, perhaps this chronic indignation is a need of your nature; it would kill me." She unceasingly combats his favourite heresy that one writes for twenty intelligent people, and that one scorns the rest. "This is not true, since absence of success irritates and affects you."

There must be no contempt for the public! One must write for all who are eager to read and are able to profit by wholesome study. There must be no proud isolation from the rest of humanity! She cannot admit that in being an artist one ceases to be oneself, and that the literary man destroys the natural man. What an extraordinary mania it is to desire, as soon as one begins to write, to be another than the real being, to be the one that disappears, the one that annihilates itself, the one that *is* not! What a false rule of taste! As for her, she tries as much as possible *to stand in the shoes of those good people.* Every author must do so if he wishes to be interesting. There is no question here of bringing one's own person forward—that is certainly useless. "But what morbid fancy is this of withdrawing one's soul from what one does? To conceal one's own opinion of the characters brought into action, and leave the reader in doubt as to what he ought to think, is to be obscure; from that moment the reader leaves one. For if he consents to listen to the story which is being told him, it is on condition that he is clearly shown that this one is a strong, that one a weak character." This was the unpardonable mistake in the *Éducation Sentimentale*, and the only cause of its failure. "The desire to depict things as they are, and the adventures of life as they represent themselves to us, is not, in my opinion, well-judged. Paint still-life as a realist or a poet, as you choose—that is quite indifferent to me. But the movements of the human heart are another matter. You cannot withdraw from that contemplation, for you are man and the reader is mankind."

Flaubert answered that he preferred a well-turned sentence to the whole science of metaphysics, and then retired in a species of jealous mystery to his worship of form. The *Journal des Goncourt* had recently given a sketch of one of the meetings of the Club of the Initiated; it drew the depressing figure of Théophile Gautier as he lovingly and ceaselessly repeated this sentence: "The form produces the idea,"—a sentence which he had that morning heard from Flaubert, and considered as the supreme formula of the school, wishing that it might be engraved on the walls. It is against this school that George Sand uses the last weapons of her dialectics, which are ever young, notwithstanding her age. These are deplorable formulæ, an exaggeration of the value of words. "In reality," she said to Flaubert, "you read, you explore, you work more than I and numbers of others do. You are a hundred times richer than any of us; you are rich, and you cry out as if you were poor. Show charity to a beggar whose mattress is full of gold, but who will only nourish himself with well-turned phrases and chosen words . . . Fool, search in your mattress and eat your gold. Nourish yourself with the ideas and feelings which are treasured up in your head and heart; words and phrases—the *form* of which you think so much will naturally proceed from your digestion. You consider it an end, it is merely an effort. Supreme impartiality is an anti-human quality; a novel must before all things be human. If it is not, no one will take pleasure in its being well-written, well-composed, and well-observed in detail. The essential thing is wanting—interest." And then comes the affectionate touch to soften the severity of the advice: "You need success after this ill-luck that has so deeply troubled you. I will tell you the conditions which will infallibly bring that success. Continue to worship the manner, but take more heed of the matter" (which in her eyes were the ideas and exact meaning of the work). "Do no consider true virtue as the commonplace of literature. Give it a representative, breathe some honesty and strength into the maniacs and idiots whom you delight to deride. Leave the cavern of the realists and return to true reality, which is made up of beauty and ugliness, dulness and brilliancy, but in which the desire for what is good finds place and employment notwithstanding."

I wished to conclude this sketch by these simple and beautiful words, which seem to give the required relief and colour. Whatever may be said of George Sand, of her adventures of every kind, of the events of idea, or other events into which the fire of her imagination brought her, lastly, of her chimeras, which at one time were carried out to absolute violence of thought, there is no doubt that as one advances in her life—pictured almost daily in her correspondence—one plainly sees the increase of the treasure of her experience and reason, her intellectual fortune, and a greater decision in the employment of that dearly-bought property. And whatever may, in future, be thought of her life and works, her letters will ever shadow forth an idealised presentment of the rare qualities which are her acknowledged sign in the literary history of the time: marvellous fecundity in conception, natural genius in style, and a proud idea of art which constitutes the probity of her talent.

CHRONOLOGICAL TABLE.

Year	Event	Synchronisms.
1804	(July 5) Birth of George Sand (Amantine-Lucile-Aurore Dupin)	Establishment of the Empire. The "Code Civil" adopted by the Legislative body.
1822	Marries M. Dudevant	Bonapartist conspiracies (Berton, Caron, *the four sergeants of La Rochelle*). Congress of Vienna. Victor Hugo publishes his "Odes et Ballades."
1831	Resides in Paris	Casimir Périer, Prime Minister. "Notre Dame de Paris" published.
	First period of her talent—Psychological.	
1832	"Indiana"; "Valentine"*	The cholera in Paris; death of Casimir Périer, George Cuvier and Champollion; the Duchess de Berry lands in France, and is arrested.
1833	"Lélia"	Law on Primary Instruction. The Duchess de Berry, set at liberty, goes to Italy.
1834	"Jacques" (influence of Gustave Planche)	Success of the French Army in Algeria. Death of General La Fayette.
1835	"Léone Léoni"; "André"	Fieschi's attempt on the life of King Louis Philippe.
1836	"Simon"; "La Marquise"; "Lavinia"; Mattea"; "Metella." Separated from her husband by decision of the Court at Bourges	Louis Napoleon Bonaparte at Strasburg. Death of Armand Carrel.
1837	"Lettres d'un Voyageur" (influence of Alfred de Musset); "Mauprat" . .	The Duc d'Orleans marries the Princess Helen of Mecklenburg-Schwerin. Treaty of La Tafna. Taking of Constantine. Opening of the Museum at Versailles.
1838	"La Dernière Aldini"; "Les Maîtres Mosaïstes"	Admiral Baudin bombards Vera Cruz. Death of Prince Talleyrand.
1839	"Spiridion" (influence of Lamennais); "L'Uscoque." Settles at Nohant .	Abd-el-Kader defeated on the Banks of La Chiffa. Daguerre invents the art of photography.
1840	"Gabriel"; "Les Sept Cordes de la Lyre" (influence of Pierre Leroux) . .	Battle of Mazagran. French successes in Algeria. Marriage of the Duc de Nemours.
	Second period of her talent—Political.	
1841	"Le Compagnon du Tour de France" (influence of Michel de Bourges) . .	Treaty of the Quadruple Alliance. Treaty with Holland.

1842	"Horace" (influence of Michel de Bourges); "Consuelo".	Death of the Duc d'Orleans.
1843	"La Comtesse de Rudolstadt".	The Queen of England visits France.
1845	"Le Meunier d'Angibault" (influence of Pierre Leroux)	Negotiations with England about the right of search.
1846	"La Mare au Diable"	Louis Napoleon escapes from his prison at Ham. Marriages of the Duc de Montpensier and the Duc de Bordeaux.
1847	"Le Péché de M. Antoine" (influence of Michel de Bourges)	The Duc d'Aumale appointed Governor of Algeria. M. de Lamartine publishes his "Histoire des Girondins."
	Third period of her talent—Idyllic.	
1848	"La petite Fadette"; "François le Champi"	Republic in France; civil war. Riot of 23-26 June. Death of Châteaubriand.
	Takes an active part in the Revolutionary movement. "Lettres au Peuple."	
1854		Death of Lamennais.
1857	"La Daniella"; "Les Beaux Messieurs de Bois-Doré" (dramatised in 1862)	Death of General Cavaignac, of Bérenger, of Gustave Planche, and of Alfred de Musset.
1859	"L'Homme de Neige"; "Elle et Lui'	War declared against Austria.
	Fourth period of her talent—Psychological.	
1861	"Le Marquis de Villemer" (dramatised in 1864); "Valvèdre."	
1863	"Mademoiselle de La Quintinie."	
1876	"Flamarande."	
,,	(June 8th) Death of George Sand.	

* We have thought it necessary to give the dates of only the principal works of George Sand.

INDEX.